CW00958706

The Royal Race

The Royal Race

for the British Crown

JILLIAN ROBERTSON

Blond & Briggs

First published 1977 by Blond & Briggs Ltd, London, and Tiptree, Colchester, Essex © copyright 1977 Jillian Robertson. Printed in Great Britain by The Anchor Press Ltd and bound by Wm Brendon & Son Ltd, both of Tiptree, Essex. SBN 85634 068 5

Thank you to:
>
> Julian Bell
>
> Anthony Mockler
>
> Jonathan Guinness
>
> Milton Shulman
>
> Donald Horne, who was my first editor
>
> Dr Monica Felton
>
> and my son Jamie Page who helped with
> the guide to the houses

The author also wishes to acknowledge the gracious permission of Her Majesty the Queen; the Directors of the Wallace Collection; the Board of General Purposes, United Grand Lodge of England; R. Page Croft Esq. of Ware, Hertfordshire; and the Governors of Claremont School, to reproduce the photographs in this book.

List of Illustrations

Contents

George III is Still Winning

1817. America was lost. Waterloo was won. Napoleon was imprisoned on St Helena. The winner, King George III, was a prisoner in Windsor Castle. England was in a wretched state. The failure of the crops and the stagnation of trade which followed peace caused distress in the working classes. Riotous meetings, excesses and seditious risings threatened the country with insurrection. Prisons were full. Rioters and robbers were flogged and hanged. Convicts were sent in chains to New South Wales. Memories of French Revolution mobs were fresh and in February a nervous Parliament suspended Habeas Corpus. Hope for peace relied on the better rule to come when the King's only grandchild, Princess Charlotte, would become sovereign.

The King, 'Farmer George', now nearing eighty years old, totally blind, almost deaf, witless and suffering from porphyria and illusions, had been insane on and off for twenty years. He had been locked away in two lower rooms at Windsor Castle where his loud laughter echoed through the corridors. He had just had his snowy white beard, which flowed down over his purple dressing-gown, cut off. No one had spoken to him for years, for voices put him in a frenzy; he was no longer part of that world which he had found so difficult, so alien. He was seldom violent now.

He conversed with the dead. 'They say it is a most charming illusion,' said one courtier. He chattered incessantly to phantoms of his past and his good friend, King Lear. As he played soothing hymns on his harpsichord he was unaware that his sometime ambition to keep his family – the Hanoverian House of Brunswick – the most exclusively royal and Protestant in the world, had almost condemned them to extinction.

*　　　*　　　*

I
Prinny
1795–1817

In 1795 labourers were being transported to Australia for demanding a wage of 2s 6d a day and the eldest son of George III, the Prince of Wales, was sent to the altar for debts of £650,000. The only way to pay for his appetites for twelve-course dinners, elegance, fun, diamonds, sex, houses and horses was to marry, as Parliament was obliged to increase his allowance to £125,000 per annum once he had a princess to support 'to keep up the splendour of the illustrious House of Brunswick'. The Prince was only truthful when it was convenient, so his secret but, in the eyes of many, legal marriage ten years earlier to the Roman Catholic widow Mrs Fitzherbert, was ignored so he could marry officially and get some of his debts paid off by Parliament. Solemnised legally by a Church of England curate in Mayfair in 1785, this marriage, if regular, would have disqualified the Prince of Wales from becoming King because of the 1689 Bill of Rights and the Act of Settlement of 1701 which barred any Roman Catholic or any heir married to a Roman Catholic from coming to the throne. At the time of the Fitzherbert/Prince of Wales wedding James II's grandson, the Catholic 'Bonnie Prince Charlie' – the Young Pretender – had assumed the title Charles III of Great Britain and had retired to Florence. The Stuart supporters, the Jacobites, were always looking for an excuse to push the Protestant Hanoverians from the throne and the Prince of Wales certainly put his inheritance at risk. The position remains the same today: no one married to a Roman Catholic can ascend the throne.

Mrs Fitzherbert had buried her two earlier husbands; now she watched while her third arranged bigamy. But she had dignity.

She deposited the royal wedding certificate at Coutts Bank and retired to her house in Battersea and her retreat on the Steine at Brighton, with £3000 a year 'pin-money' from her husband. An emissary went to Germany to find a princess. 'One damned German frau is as good as another,' said the Prince. But when his cousin, Caroline of Brunswick, arrived in England three days before the planned wedding, she was worse than he'd expected. 'I am not well,' he said. 'Pray get me a glass of brandy.' Caroline was grubby, untidy and had a distinct odour. Nor did Caroline like the look of her new husband. 'I find him very fat and not half as handsome as his portrait,' she commented to Lord Malmesbury, the emissary who had found her.

The Prince of Wales was drunk during the brief wedding ceremony on 8 April and had to be supported by the Duke of Bedford. His 'sloven' of a bride, gauche and red-faced, also nearly fell over – not because of alcohol but because her court dress was so richly embroidered and embossed and stiffened that the weight of it made her topple. The drunk groom 'shed tears' when the Archbishop of Canterbury asked twice whether there was any impediment to lawful marriage and waited for a reply. The Archbishop gabbled through the perilous injunction. Despite his revulsion the Prince managed to consummate his bigamous marriage. Later Caroline told Lady Bury that the Prince spent the night 'under the grate where he fell and where I left him'.

The reluctant bridegroom took his new wife to Kempshott House in Hampshire for their honeymoon. He chose Kempshott because it had previously belonged to Mrs Fitzherbert and, to add an element of perversity, he took along his current mistress, Lady Jersey, whom he had made into one of his wife's Ladies-in-Waiting. He also had drinking companions staying at Kempshott House who spent their days 'sleeping and snoring in their boots on the sofa'.

* * *

Nine months later, on 7 January 1796, the Prince of Wales announced:

'The Princess, after a terrible hard labour for above twelve hours is this instant brought to bed of an immense Girl and I assure you, notwithstanding we might have wish'd for a Boy, I receive her with all the Affection possible.'

The Prince of Wales thought Princess Charlotte Augusta's birth was sufficient to safeguard 'the glorious House of Hanover and the Protestant succession', and six months after the birth a formal separation letter was sent by the Prince of Wales to his wife, Caroline. Now that he was free, he returned to Mrs Fitzherbert – after the Pope gave her permission to resume the 'marriage'. The Papal Brief from Rome declared that the Supreme Pontiff pronounced Mrs Fitzherbert to be the wife of the Prince of Wales according to the law of the Roman Catholic Church; she was, therefore, free to rejoin her husband if he were truly 'penitent for his sins and sincere in his promises of amendment'. So the Fitzherbert marriage resumed in June 1799.

The Prince of Wales' other wife – Caroline, Princess of Wales – with her painted eyebrows, circus-like rouged cheeks, oozing breasts, bizarre clothes and wanton manners, became the acid enemy of her dandy husband. The Prince's ambition to divorce her bordered on monomania. Divorce meant death to Caroline. 'The crime of adultery on her part must be proved in an English court of justice,' the Duke of Kent told the diarist Creevey. 'And if found guilty she must be executed for High Treason!' (Even today adultery by the wife of the monarch's eldest son is high treason.)

The Prince of Wales' extreme hatred of his official wife tainted his relationship with the daughter conceived after what he alleged was their only act of copulation together. The Prince wanted to marry again and have sons to deprive Charlotte of the succession, as the idea of any child of 'the vilest wretch on earth' sitting on the throne was abhorrent to him. He would often angrily demand, 'Damn the West! And Damn the East! The question is how am I to get rid of this Damned Princess of Wales?'

The Prince – 'Prinny' – had little self-restraint and all his life was burdened with too much fat and too many debts. He was a

heavy drinker and towards the end of his life he became addicted
to opium. He was frequently hysterical and given to over-dramatisation. His extravagances were staggering: he bought suits by the
dozen, shirts by the score, toothbrushes by the hundred, pocketbooks by the five hundred, whips by the hundred. In need of a
walking-stick he bought thirty-two in one day. He had at least
eight field-marshal's full-dress uniforms and the accoutrements
of all the orders in Europe. Vain and self-indulgent, he was none
the less a perfect gentleman and could remain courteous and
polished even when mixing with undesirables.

Charles Greville later described the Prince's existence:

'He leads a most extraordinary life – never gets up till six in the
afternoon. They come to him and open the window curtains at
six or seven o'clock in the morning; he breakfasts in bed, does
whatever business he can be brought to transact in bed too, he
reads every newspaper quite through, dozes three or four hours,
gets up in time for dinner, and goes to bed between ten and
eleven. He sleeps very ill, and rings his bell forty times in the
night; if he wants to know the hour, though a watch hangs
close to him, he will have his valet de chambre down rather
than turn his head to look at it. The same thing if he wants a
glass of water; he won't stretch out his hand to get it. His
valets are nearly destroyed.'

But, besides being as self-indulgent as a fairy-tale emperor,
he was a highly civilised man. He was extremely knowledgeable,
particularly about art, literature and music, and could hold his own
with classical scholars. He was such a comic and wit that he could
have had a career on the stage. He did everything in style. For
example, when on the second anniversary of Waterloo he was
to open the new Strand Bridge – London's fourth – he went
down the Thames in his crimson and scarlet barge. He had already
had the river decorated with boats in bunting and gigantic flags.
His inventive taste extended to mammoth building schemes by
his friend 'Flash' Nash who built Regent Street which now extended from Piccadilly in a majestic sweep towards the Marylebone fields where Doric-pillared crescents were being laid out. He

bought pictures by the score so that now the Royal Family have the most valuable collection of paintings in the world. He didn't just *buy*; he knew *what* to buy.

But he also vacillated. His orders and decisions followed his changing moods so very quickly that everything about him was contradictory. He was repellent and disarming, intolerable and irresistible. He was an affectionate and delightful brother to his spinster sisters, yet as a father he was abominable.

When his daughter was eleven, the Prince of Wales was left by the woman he described in his will as 'his lawful wife, Mrs Fitzherbert', and he made his first public attempt to divorce his official wife, Caroline, via the so-called 'Delicate Investigation'. A tribunal sat at 10 Downing Street on 1 June 1806 and heard evidence that the ludicrous Caroline had committed adultery and that the child she had adopted, William Austin, was her own illegitimate offspring. The hearing turned out to be a lewd pantomime of ribaldry and indecorum. After a month of hearing a procession of witnesses – dressers, pages, housemaids, laundresses, apothecaries, footmen and friends – making sworn statements, the tribunal reluctantly cleared Caroline.

Evidence against her stuck. A manservant, Robert Cole, said 'she grew lusty and appeared large behind'. Her footman, Roberts, declared that 'the Princess was very fond of fucking'. Another witness said she had made love to the artist Thomas Lawrence. Someone else told of the mechanical doll that performed obscene acts after dinner.

A nervous government averted its gaze from this accusation of horizontal high treason between the sheets. Although the verdict was 'not proven', Caroline was ostracised by much of Society and the Prince of Wales declined to attend any function where he might meet his wife. Queen Charlotte decided that she and the King could no longer receive their niece and daughter-in-law.

Opinion was divided. Some sided with the 'injured' Princess, others with the furious Prince. His attempt to have his wife disgraced and divorced made him more odious to the mob who heaped sympathy on the persecuted Princess of Wales and her daughter. Charlotte, brought up by a group of aristocratic governesses headed by the Dowager Lady Elgin, in Warwick House, had never lived under the same roof as either her father or her mother since the age of two. She led a restrained childhood with 'visits of maternal tenderness once a week'. She had no one to give her day-to-day love except a hired help.

The Prince kept Charlotte in obscurity. Lord Brougham assured Lord Grey in 1813 that: 'He is jealous of her (Charlotte) to a degree of insanity, and has been for some time. While his carriage was met by stony silence or hisses, Charlotte's was saluted by cheers and hurrahs.'

Her face still slightly marked by childhood smallpox, her brows and lashes pale, her blue eyes protuberant in the Hanoverian way, her figure over-ripe, Charlotte at eighteen was no beauty. But her lively expression and a hearty manner – except when displaying 'the fixed stare of the House of Brunswick' – made her attractive. She was so vivacious that critics said she was overbearing and contradictory. The Duke of Wellington was irritated by her familiarity – she addressed him as 'Arthur'. She exasperated others by giving glimpses of her fine pair of legs which, like her father, she delighted to show, or her loud chats at church in between prayers and the sermon. Her conversation was punctuated by 'Oh Lord' and 'Oh, God'.

'Her hands generally folded behind her, her body always pushed forward, never standing quiet, from time to time stamping her foot, laughing a great deal, and talking still more . . .' was how Stockmar described her in his memoirs.

Dr Matthew Baillie, the Royal Physician, encouraged her riding to counter her tendency to stoutness – an easy command as she was buckish about horses and rode fast over rough paddocks and even disguised herself as a cavalry officer, galloping legs astride, around Windsor. She turned 'corners at a gallop and stopped short of the horse's tail'. By contrast 'my dearest papa', now slimmed down to a mere nineteen or twenty stone, had to be hoisted onto his horse by a winch because of his fifty-five-inch waist and his gout.

Like many Hanoverians, Charlotte was a hearty eater and would ask with gusto for 'cold beef and plenty of mustard'. When at Bognor, she tripped down to Richardson's the bakers, when the buns were due out of the oven. She would buy some hot and eat them over the counter, chatting to Richardson.

In the 'Age of Elegance', Charlotte did not fetter herself with tiresome ceremonies and, except for court occasions, dressed much like a successful tradesman's wife, adding wreaths of artificial roses to decorate her thin, blonde, curly hair.

Charlotte endeared herself to the Whigs who referred to her as 'the young'un'. When her plight – thanks to her father's heavy hand – became a public scandal, the Whigs asked questions in Parliament. Lord Byron, outraged by the Prince of Wales' harshness towards Charlotte, wrote a poem:

> '. . . Weep daughter of a royal line,
> A sire's disgrace,
> A realm's decay . . .'

Anxious to rid himself of this insubordinate daughter the Regent was determined to marry her off to the Protestant William of Orange, who had been educated at Oxford, served with Wellington and lived across the Channel. This Princeling was heir to the Dutch throne, with which the government wanted an alliance, and, according to Wellington, was 'dissolute, untidy and stupid'.

His physique was so frail that he was known by everyone as 'Slender Billy'. He had buck-teeth, a sallow appearance, a violent handshake and a swaying spine when he drank. He often drank too much.

'I think him so ugly,' commented Charlotte after their first meeting, 'that I am sometimes obliged to turn my head away in disgust when he is speaking to me. Marry I will, and that directly, in order to enjoy my liberty; but not the Prince of Orange.'

But she suppressed her revulsion. Before Christmas 1814, Charlotte agreed to marry Slender Billy and, after an exchange of rings and portraits, was engaged for six months. However, when the marriage contract was drawn up, it stipulated that she would live part of every year in Holland. Charlotte was frightened: if she was absent abroad her father would really divorce her mother, remarry, beget a male heir and oust her from the throne. She broke off the engagement. Charlotte was now passionate *not* to marry the Prince of Orange; she wanted to be Queen of England. The real danger lay in the extreme Protestant party in England and Wales who disapproved of Roman Catholics, of the Prince of Wales' behaviour and the Royal Marriages Act. If they exposed her father's wedding to Roman Catholic Mrs Fitzherbert and, therefore, the illegality of his marriage to her mother, Charlotte would be illegitimate and disqualified from the throne. To guard her position, she declared that she would never step off English soil.

The wedding guest list was sent to Charlotte by her father, and of course, did not include her mother's name. Charlotte returned it with her own erased. The Regent raged. On 12 July he stormed into Warwick House and informed her that her personal attendants – whom he suspected of influencing her against the Prince of Orange – were dismissed, that she was to be confined at Carlton House for five days and then taken to Cranbourne Lodge in Windsor Forest. Charlotte ran out of the house crying, rushed past her sentries and hailed a hackney coach off the Strand at Charing Cross. She sped to her mother's house in Connaught Place and only returned after a document was signed by her father which stated that the proposed marriage with the Prince of Orange would never take place.

Charlotte paid the price of her victory; her punishment was to become a prisoner in Windsor Forest. She was allowed no visitors, apart from those on a short list approved by her father, and the only outings permitted (other than riding) were visits to her overbearing grandmother's dull musical evenings or family evenings where the four spinster princesses played cards or 'Snip Snap Snorum', a card game invented by themselves.

'I dislike two things,' she said; 'apple pie and my grandmother.' Brougham asked in Parliament, 'Why again is the Princess to be treated as a state criminal? Why are we to have a Queen so brought up? Out of Turkey is there anything so barbarous?'

Six months after Charlotte broke off the engagement, the tension between father and daughter eased and they celebrated Christmas together. The Prince of Wales again asked her to marry William of Orange. Again she refused but suggested Prince

Leopold of Saxe-Coburg as a substitute. This minor German prince was one of the seven children of the energetic and affectionate Duchess Augusta of Saxe-Coburg Gotha, widow of the Duke who ruled this pocket-handkerchief duchy. He was so poor that when he'd visited London for the Victory celebrations he had lived in rented lodgings over a grocer's shop in Marylebone High Street. But he had dark good looks. 'If I end by marrying Leopold, I marry the best of all those I have seen,' wrote Charlotte to a friend, 'and that is some satisfaction.'

Most saw him as a talented soldier but the Regent dismissed him as a calculating careerist and nicknamed him '*le Marquis peu a peu*'. Other comments were: 'He is a damned humbug' and 'He was a little unctuous and shifty and did not look at the person to whom he was talking.'

Yet the Regent agreed to the wedding.

Leopold was doted on by his mother, who was distressed at the geographical distance about to separate her from her adored son. 'I realise only too well what this marriage entails – Leopold's complete severance from his former existence and from us all. The parting . . . (and) the sea will form a barrier . . .'

On 19 February 1816, storms caused Leopold's crossing of the Channel on the luxurious *Royal Sovereign*, the Regent's yacht, to take seven hours. On account of the ebb tide the boat could not enter the harbour and they had to go ashore in a *chaloupe*. He travelled to Brighton, the guest of the Prince Regent at the exotic domed pavilion where he met his future wife again. A marriage contract was drawn up and a Bill for the naturalisation of the groom was passed with unprecedented speed; it was read, debated, went through both Houses, and received the Royal Assent all in one evening.

He was not only being accepted by Parliament; according to the popular satirist, Peter Pindar, in *Wooing and Cooing*, he had got into 'a pickle most distressing' with a 'belle most beauteous and fair' and at Brighton:

> '*The youth had time to think at leisure*
> *On those hot passions which beguile*
> *The body into evil pleasure.*'

[19]

When Leopold did not attend the Queen's Drawing Room, Peter Pindar hinted at a sinister cause for his absence:

> *'Some swore High Highness was grown coy*
> *Others threw out he was infected:*
> *A few the slander heard with joy,*
> *And others the foul thought rejected.'*

Owing to twelve-course dinners at the pavilion, Leopold was 'attacked by severe rheumatic pains in the head'. Peter Pindar goes on to muse that Prinny found Leopold 'uncommon thin' and plied him with beef and punch to fatten him up:

> *'His nose was long, his eyes were grey*
> *His phiz was somewhat thin and sallow*
> *His locks were brown: – a lightish bay –*
> *His teeth irregular and yellow.'*

But at last Charlotte was married. Leopold's mother wrote in her diary: 'Oh, God has chosen this fate for Leopold, and has ordained that he should in time share the perils that beset a crowned head . . .'

The largest throng of spectators ever seen jammed into St James's Park, the Mall and nearby streets to watch the wedding on 2 May 1816. Even 'trees were filled'. The ceremony went smoothly until Leopold uttered: 'And with my worldly goods I thee endow', at which Charlotte burst into giggles, for he was penniless. Parliament had voted them a joint income of £60,000 a year, money for setting up house and a pension of £50,000 for Leopold if he outlived Charlotte. Guns were fired across England, and in Coburg a salute of guns was fired and a thanksgiving service was held to celebrate the union of the House of Brunswick with the House of Coburg. The children of this union would be the future monarchs of England. The future Royal Family of England would be the House of Saxe-Coburg.

After a brief honeymoon with the Duchess of York and her forty dogs at Oatlands, the couple spent the summer at Camelford House in Oxford Street. They were cheered and mobbed on their visits to the theatre and on outings. When Leopold

pedantically corrected Charlotte's ungainliness and impetuosity
she would smile and promise that he would never, never have to
reprove her again.

On 30 July bulletins announced Charlotte's immediate recovery
from a miscarriage.

In August, covered military wagons moved the couple's
possessions to Claremont House, Esher, a lavish, colonnaded
Palladian mansion with sixteen main rooms – purchased for them
by the State for a bargain £69,000. Designed by the great land-
scape gardener, Capability Brown, at limitless cost for Lord
Clive, 'Conqueror of India', it was strangely disquieting. Since
Clive's suicide forty-two years earlier – when he had locked
himself in a lavatory and slit his throat with a pocket-knife in his
Berkeley Square house – Claremont had had four different owners.
The house was sold to the Crown Estates for Charlotte by Charles
Rose Ellis after his wife died there in childbirth. Jane Austen
visited Claremont in 1813 and wrote that the house seemed 'never
to have prospered'.

In the freezing winter of 1816–17 Charlotte and Leopold lived
quietly at Claremont – he addressed her as 'Chaaaaarlott' with a
guttural German accent, and she called him 'my love'. They
breakfasted together at 11.00 and occasionally had friends or
relatives – including the Duke of Sussex, the Duke of York and
the Grand Duke Nicolas of Russia, and Charlotte's friend the
Princess Lieven – to dinner at 7.00. There were no lavish parties
and the largest room in the house, the sixty-foot gallery which
housed Clive's spectacular Indian carpet, was never used. Even in
the house, Charlotte and Leopold walked arm in arm. They read,
sang duets on the new Broadwood piano (one of a pair – the other
went to Beethoven), sharing the same stool, and studied.

The Comtesse de Boigne visited Claremont when Charlotte
was pregnant.

'After waiting a very long time we heard a loud and echoing
step in the neighbouring rooms, which I can only compare
with the tramp of a drum-major. People about me said, "Here
is the Princess". She was evidently anxious to imitate "The

[21]

Great Elizabeth" with the intentionally heavy step and the haughty carriage of her head. . . .'

When she sat down to dinner and could not see her husband who was obscured by a silver centre-piece the Princess summoned up courage and had the ornament taken off the table.

Charlotte's devotion to Leopold was immense. Until her marriage, she had suffered much emotional stress as a result of the bitter and intractable quarrel between her father and mother. She had had a lonely and secluded life dependent on governesses and tutors instead of parental love. Sir Richard Croft, the obstetrician, wrote to his sister, after one of his early visits to Claremont:

'They leave us about half-past ten and he reads to her every night till twelve . . . I was with him alone for three hours the other day . . . he told me he never knew what it was to be in debt, though he had been accustomed to a very small income, and that he determined on three things when he married – never to be in debt, not to ask for favours, and not to become a party man. . . .'

Leopold was having much difficulty in acquiring a clear English accent. Much time was spent strolling in the gardens, the park, and sitting near the artificial lake. They both were passionate amateur gardeners and botanists. Botany was the rage among the aristocrats and gentry in England in the early nineteenth century – Queen Charlotte and her daughters drew every specimen at Kew. The Royal Family did for plants then what the present Royal Family have done for horses. It was fashionable to be interested in nature.

'We knew each other,' Leopold said later. 'We were together always except when I went out to shoot. And we could be together, we did not tire. She was always thinking of others, not of herself. Oh, what happiness was ours – and it was solid.' The Princess – with her own hands – took the Prince's linen from the drawer to air when he was out shooting and even folded his cravat and saw that hot water was ready for his use, and personally prepared refreshment for his return.

The year before her marriage Charlotte had debts of £20,000 but under Leopold's direction she paid bills promptly. 'When you come on the first Monday of the month you will always find us employed in the same manner,' Charlotte told a visitor who found her table covered with bills and household accounts. 'We are determined to live within our income, and not get into debt...' She jokingly referred to her husband and herself as 'Mr and Mrs Coburg'.

The economic decline of the country, which caused much starvation and unemployment, provoked the Princess into stimulating oppressed industries. After the Spitalfield riots she ordered 2000 yards of silk from the mills there. The suffering in Worcester inspired her to order an elaborate dinner service. Huish, writing in 1818, says: 'In Claremont nothing foreign was to be seen. Much as she admired Dresden and Sèvres chinaware she would not admit a single article of it.'

When Charlotte moved to Claremont several butchers applied to supply meat to the household. When told that they were men of substance and respectability Charlotte enquired if there were other butchers in Esher. Only one, her steward told her, but he was in low circumstances and couldn't take a Royal contract. Charlotte met the poor butcher, lent him money to go into the market upon equal terms with his competitors, and gave him the Royal meat contract. When Mrs Griffiths, the future nurse, who had 'been in the habit of attending the first families in the country upon similar occasions, for about thirty years', first visited Claremont, the Prince and Princess stood talking to her for half an hour with their arms linked. 'Now, Mrs Griffiths, you will procure the baby-linen wherever you think proper, except from Mrs ————', commanded Charlotte. 'For every person that has been to see me has so pestered me with recommendations in her favour, that I am determined not to be persuaded into anything.' Then she added, 'I wish you to be here sometime before you will be wanted, that myself and this dear love' (looking at Leopold) 'may become friends with you.'

Another example of her determination was reported in the *Sunday Times*. Prince Leopold was being painted in his Garter

Robes and the artist improved his legs. Charlotte rose earlier than usual one morning and 'taking up the first brush which came in her way, she, in two or three minutes, effectually removed every trace of the Prince's legs . . .' She replied 'that she disliked flattery in any shape and moreover as she admired her Lord and Prince such as he was above all other men no representations of HRH could meet with her approbation if it differed from the original.' The legs were repainted in their imperfection.

Years later Leopold wrote: 'Our rule was never to permit one single day to pass over *ein missverstandnis* (misunderstanding) however trifling.'

But all was not paradise. On 10 October 1817, a week before her baby was due, Charlotte wrote to her mother who had been abroad for three years. Like her father, she suffered from hysterical depression. But many historians think this letter is not authentic and believe it was a fake put out by aides of the Princess of Wales to help defend her case against divorce. Only a copy is in the Royal Archives:

'My dearest mother.
A very few days may elapse before I may claim to be addressed by the endearing appellation with which I have commenced this letter . . . But, oh my mother! when my timid imagination revolves upon the uncertainty which veils futurity – when I look to the dark probabilities which may put a period to the claim of hope, even shadows shake my courage, and I feel myself the victim of terrors which reason would almost demonstrate absurd . . . I have no friend, no relation near me . . . with a single exception . . . I fear less to die than to live, the prospect of protracted existence is so blended with dangers and difficulties; so shadowed with clouds and uncertainties, so replete with anxieties and apprehensions that I must shrink from the contemplation of it, and fly for refuge even to the probability of my removal from so joyless an inheritance . . . Death would obliterate no image of delight from my heart . . .'

*   *   *

II

The Baby is Rubbed with Mustard

November 1817

The King was in his straitwaist jacket at Windsor with his phantoms; his son, the Prince Regent, was in his corsets holidaying with his mistress Lady Hertford; and Mrs Bickers, the gamekeeper's wife, was at the Claremont lodge with milk in her breasts waiting to become Royal wet nurse to the future king. The nurse, Mrs Griffiths, had arrived in an autumn drizzle at Claremont House. At Esher, two miles from the small colonnaded mansion in the Surrey hills, newspaper correspondents at the Bear Inn were dispatching news of the lying-in to an eager and expectant populace. At Dover Castle the Navy stood by to fire Congreve rockets to announce the first Royal birth for a generation. Huge bonfires had been prepared all over the English countryside; still they were unlit and now damp in the fog.

On 9 October 1817, newspapers reported that the infant was 'expected in nine or ten days' time'. Sir Richard Croft, Princess Charlotte's obstetrician, took up residence at Claremont, and the Archbishop of Canterbury moved to Fulham Palace so he could speed to the confinement when summoned.

But on 1 November there were still no signs of the arrival of the successor to the most illustrious throne in the world. The twenty-one-year-old Princess – always lumpy – was now so enormous that even her overweight grandmother, the Queen, was alarmed. When asked why her belly was not supported by corsets, Sir Richard merely said: 'A cow does not wear stays; why should the Princess Charlotte?' This progressive physician forbade Charlotte red meat or red wine 'to reduce her morbid excess of animal spirits'.

Croft's directions were simple. She was to rise at nine and take breakfast before ten; to eat a little cold meat, or some fruit and bread at lunch about two; to take food plainly cooked and easy of digestion at dinner; to take exercise, both walking and on horseback, every day that the weather was fine, but the exercise should not be violent; to use the shower bath every other day and to begin with the water tepid, and to have the loins sponged with cold water daily.

In those days when bleeding was a panacea for all ills Charlotte was sometimes bled. In a letter of 10 August to Croft, she writes: 'I am certainly much the better for the bleeding.' On one occasion four incisions were made in the arm without effect as the veins were so deeply buried. The blood was eventually withdrawn from a vein at the back of the hand where it had frequently been taken before.

England was on tip-toes with expectation. The prolonged wait heightened the people's obsession with the Prince Regent's only daughter and the King's only grandchild. Enormous sums were gambled on the sex of the expected child, and it was calculated that a Princess would only raise shares two and a half per cent, whilst a Prince would send them up six per cent. The country, suffering from its worst ever economic recession, turned with relief to the irrepressible, noisy Princess Charlotte. Most of the Royal Family was detested. The English had long placed their hopes on 'their star of promise' who would, when Queen, supercede the existing tyranny by a better form of government.

The dizzy euphoria that had swept the land after the Battle of Waterloo – only two years earlier – had been replaced by starvation, despair and riots. Streets swarmed with beggars. The harvests of 1816 had failed owing to the torrential rains, and prices soared as law and order toppled. With the fall of Napoleon England had emerged as the most powerful nation in the world. But the peace without plenty caused burning, machinery-wrecking and looting. The Regent and his government took a firm stand, for he feared 'the Revolution' and said these riots were proof of incipient Jacobinism. The mob responded with hissing and hatred, though cheering for their heroine Charlotte who had been mistreated and neglected by that monster, her father.

Two days after her baby was due, three or four bulletins issued daily increased newspaper sales:

'October 21, Claremont, 4 o'clock: . . . Her Royal Highness accompanies His Serene Highness through their domains sometimes walking, at others riding by his side for hours . . .'

'October 22, Claremont, 5 o'clock: . . . The foggy and damp weather improved and HRH walked in the garden to view the improvements that are being made there under HRH's arrangement and direction . . .'

With a deep sigh, labour pains began a fortnight late. The waters broke at 5.15 p.m. Contractions followed soon after. These, though only gentle and ineffectual, continued through the night and at 3.15 the next morning, fast horses were dispatched. For three weeks footmen had waited in riding-dress and horses had been saddled day and night ready to gallop the sixteen miles to London to alert the Privy Councillors and Prelates who were to attest the birth of the future monarch.

The first to arrive was the Earl Bathurst, President of the Board of Trade, from his seat at Putney at 5.15 in the freezing pre-dawn. Half an hour later Viscount Sidmouth, the prudish and conscientious Home Secretary, arrived from Richmond Park. Fifteen minutes later, the Archbishop of Canterbury and the Bishop of London stepped out of their carriage. Next came the Princess's physician, little Dr Baillie, in a chariot and four at 7.15 a.m. Nicolas Vansittart, the Chancellor of the Exchequer, was not so quick. A chariot and four brought him from Downing Street at 7.30 a.m. Last was Lord Eldon, the Lord Chancellor, who came in a chaise from Bedford Square and whom the Royal Family called 'Old Bags'. Charlotte so loathed him that she had once declared she'd never speak to him again. He had once told her father, 'If she was my daughter I'd lock her up.'

The six distinguished men waited hour after hour in the breakfast room with the Princess's green parrot, Coco. These Tory ministers whom Charlotte so disliked – she was a passionate Whig – were only separated from her by the double door to her bedroom. Charlotte and Leopold paced their twenty-five-foot room warmed by the wood fire in the yellow and white marble fireplace.

'I will neither shriek nor yell,' Charlotte declared to Griffiths, the nurse. Sir Richard had never seen such 'resolution and firmness' as her labour lasted for fifty-two hours and she never 'uttered a murmur' of complaint.

The labour was so slow that it was not until 5.30 p.m. on Tuesday – a full day after the onset of contractions – that she was put to bed. Her beloved Leopold sometimes lay down beside her and always held her hand. But the pains ceased once she lay down, and again Charlotte had to march up and down, up and down the bedroom, leaning on Leopold. He exclaimed to the doctors in his guttural German accent: '. . . that the unrepining, patient endurance of the Princess, whilst it gives me comfort, communicates also a deep affliction at her suffering being so lengthened.'

Again and again she climbed up the wooden two-tier bedsteps into the four-poster hung with flowered chintz, lined with pink cambric, which was placed between the only two windows in the room.

The infant was in an awkward, unfavourable position. Three hours after the 'putting to bed' the use of forceps was discussed. Before Lord Lister's introduction of sterile conditions in surgery mortality was high when instruments instead of hands were used. A letter summoning Dr John Sims, an expert in instrument births, was written on Tuesday morning, but not sent until nine o'clock on Tuesday evening, so he did not arrive till two o'clock on Wednesday morning.

Croft became nervous. He often was over-anxious and now he was attending the most important woman, dynastically, in the world – the future monarch of the country that was supreme.

The mile-long driveway at Claremont was busy with messengers on horseback. Progress reports went to the Prime Minister, Lord Liverpool, and to the Prince Regent who was at his shoot over 100 miles north in Suffolk. Even though she was in extreme pain each bulletin declared: 'HRH is doing extremely well.' Messages became so optimistic that *The Times* held back an edition for two hours on the Wednesday, hoping to announce the birth. But the baby refused to come. Everyone was weary. Charlotte was weak from lack of food. Croft said: 'It is better for you not to eat.' Leopold stayed with his wife but seldom spoke and was often on the point of collapse.

When Dr Sims arrived with his forceps he was never allowed to see the Princess as Croft said: 'Being unknown to the Princess, his appearance might have alarmed her.' So Sims and Baillie acted solely as advisers and never got closer to the Princess than Leopold's dressing-room door, although their names were affixed to the bulletins. Dr Baillie had been Charlotte's personal physician for years, yet he was not allowed by Croft to see her.

At six on Wednesday night Croft said he could still hear the foetal heartbeat and issued the sixth medical bulletin that day: 'The labour . . . has within the last three or four hours considerably advanced and will, it is hoped, within a few hours, be happily completed.'

At nine o'clock the Prince was born – dead. Croft rushed the warm infant into the dressing-room where Baillie and Sims plunged it into near-boiling water and rubbed mustard and vinegar onto its limbs. The doctor huffed and puffed into the motionless mouth. If they could reanimate the by then cold, lifeless boy, one day he would be king. Every medical and folklore trick was tried. The suspense was too great – he was almost alive, almost. But the unborn King had suffocated in the womb. When resuscitation failed, the dead Prince, wrapped in white shawls, was carried by the weeping nurse, followed by Croft, into the breakfast-room to meet the Great Officers of State.

'A noble infant it was,' wrote Lord Eldon, 'as like the Royal Family as possible.' Vansittart said the child's head had been squeezed out of shape. Most comments were about the excessive size of the baby, 'having the appearance of a child ten days old.'

Leopold in his fractured English exclaimed: 'Than Godt, Than Godt, zee Princess is zafe.' Charlotte was calm: 'It is the will of

God, and it is our duty to submit,' she said. And she assured her attendants: 'God bless you; I thank you for all your attentions.'

Sudden bleeding caused Croft to remove the afterbirth manually, but the Princess was easy and animated. She broke her fast with chicken broth, a little gruel, some toast and barley water. She threw up some cardiac medicine – camphor julep.

At eleven o'clock the exhausted Ministers and Prelates left, assured that the Princess was well. The doctors went to bed, Croft lying in his clothes in Leopold's dressing-room. Still Charlotte did not sleep. She was hyper-cheerful. 'How smart you are, Griffiths,' she remarked gaily when the nurse changed her dress. Then, looking at Leopold who was on the bed beside her, added in the same too happy manner: 'How long do you think it will be before I shall again comb Leopold's hair?' – she always combed his black curls when he returned after shooting.

Charlotte was then drowsy from an opiate, so Leopold went to an upstairs room to sleep. But at midnight Charlotte was awake. Mrs Griffiths brought more gruel but Charlotte was unable to swallow it and vomited. She complained of singing in her head, and footmen rushed to fetch Baillie and Sims. She continued to complain of nausea and her pulse accelerated. Croft went to Baron Stockmar, Leopold's German aide and personal physician, and said, 'The Princess is dangerously ill. You must go and inform the Prince of the state of things.'

Stockmar woke Leopold but he 'did not appear to understand that the state of the Princess was very serious'. It is thought that Leopold had taken an opiate to induce sleep. They talked for fifteen minutes until Leopold slid back to sleep. Stockmar hurried downstairs where Charlotte had become quiet and her pulse less frequent. At 12.30 terrible spasms came. 'Oh, what a pain,' she said, pressing her hands to her stomach. 'It is all here.'

The doctors poured brandy and hot water down Charlotte's throat and covered her shivering body with hot flannels and water bottles. A violent pain came on her chest. The Daughter of England was dying while her husband slept. Cheerfully, but in extreme pain, she complained to Stockmar: 'They have made me tipsy.'

'She stretched out her left hand eagerly to me,' said Stockmar, 'and pressed mine twice, vehemently . . . Baillie kept giving her wine constantly'. Then Charlotte looked across the room to the doctors and asked: 'Is there any danger?' Croft told her to compose herself. Stockmar left the room and Charlotte although weak yelled: 'Stocky! Stocky!' He rushed back. At 2.30 a.m. she drew her knees up in a last convulsive movement. She was dead. No one as close to the throne had died in childbirth since Jane Seymour in 1537 – and she died of fever ten days after the confinement.

Now the fifty-five-year-old childless Duke of York was heir. Two whole royal generations had been wiped out in a night.

Stockmar rushed to wake Leopold and tell him that his wife was dead. He could not realise what had happened: he had lost his baby and his wife. On the way down to the deathbed he sank down on a hall chair while Stockmar knelt beside him; it was all a dream; it was impossible. He staggered and fell on the bedroom floor kissing the icy hands of his wife: '. . . those beautiful hands which seemed always to be looking for mine . . .' He threw himself into Stockmar's arms.

The nation mourned. Charlotte's death left them without hope of the Crown they wanted. The mad King, the dissolute Regent, the court that had grown more splendid as the people starved, had been tolerated because the nation saw an end to it all. The Regent and his brothers were elderly, and after their deaths the nation's darling, Charlotte, would make a 'new earth' for her subjects. She had been Hope. Now hope was gone. Lord Brougham wrote that it was difficult to believe how universal and genuine was the grief.

The nation's sorrow was described by Princess Lieven, one of Charlotte's closest friends, on her return from France. She wrote to her brother, Alexander:

'A very sad event has marked our return here. That charming Princess Charlotte, so richly endowed with happiness, beauty, and splendid hopes, cut off from the love of a whole people. It is impossible to find in the history of nations or families an event which has evoked such heartfelt mourning. One met in the streets people of every class in tears, the churches were full at all hours, the shops shut for a fortnight (an eloquent testimony from a shop-keeping community), and everyone from the highest to the lowest, in a state of despair which it is impossible to describe . . .'

Leopold became so distraught that daily medical bulletins were issued: 'Claremont, Nov. 7: The Prince Leopold has had a bad night, but is more composed this morning.' But on the 12th it was announced that his indisposition was increasing hourly, that he refused consolation, and suffered no one to approach him. He seemed indifferent to everything. For some reason, which is not explained in contemporary records, Leopold took against the nurse, Mrs Griffiths, and made her leave immediately. He would not allow her to stay till the funeral.

Unknown to Leopold, the Lord Chamberlain sent four surgeons – including Sir Everard Home, Sir David Dundas and Mr Barne – to open and embalm the two bodies. This was done on the command of the Prince Regent, but Leopold did not know till *after* it had been done. When told, he cried yet again; he considered embalming indelicate and disgusting. (It was a practice unknown in foreign courts.) A mixture of oils of lavender, camomile, turpentine, and vermilion was forced into the arteries. The internal organs were removed, washed and deposited in a lead-lined oak urn covered with crimson velvet. Two sackfuls of 'odoriferous flowers, herbs, and ground spices' were stuffed into Charlotte's body. Then it was enclosed in a number of linen cloth wrappers, which had been previously waxed so as to keep the body in a state of high preservation for a number of years, and it was finely covered in rich blue velvet, and tied with white satin ribbon. This was done six days after the death.

The medical practitioners also examined the bodies to ascertain 'the approximate cause' of sudden death. Although two ounces of fluid were found in Charlotte's pericardium (the region around the heart) this was not the cause. All her organs and the brain appeared sound. The cause of death remained a mystery – perhaps post-natal shock or exhaustion.

[32]

The sewn-up stuffed body lay in the Royal bedroom at Claremont for thirteen days. The weeping Leopold became hysterical,
touching and talking to his dead love. He constantly clutched a
miniature of Charlotte and part of her favourite dress 'that he
will not suffer a human being to touch'. Fourteen years later,
when he was elected King Leopold I of the Belgians, Charlotte's
watchstrap still lay on the mantelpiece in their bedroom where
she had left it; her bonnet and cape still hung on the screen where
she'd put them after their last walk; her harp was never played
again. After the funeral Leopold always slept in the chintz cur-
tained four-poster where Charlotte had died; a wax cast of
Charlotte's arm and hand clasped in his rested on a nearby table.

The bodies were finally taken away at six o'clock in the evening
of 18 November. First the crimson coffin of the unnamed
Prince was carried out, followed by a large velvet-covered urn
containing his heart. Charlotte's crimson coffin studded with gold
was then borne to another black-plumed hearse. A third mourning
coach drawn by six more black horses was occupied by Leopold
with Dr Short in canonical dress. Escorted by a full company of
10th Dragoons and preceded by thirty horsemen in black, the
funeral procession moved at foot pace to Windsor. Great num-
bers followed the hearse and roads were thronged with weeping
spectators. Every house was draped in black. The melancholy
procession arrived at Windsor shortly after midnight in silent awe
under the glow of thousands of flares. The mourning coaches
slowly lumbered up the hill.

Charlotte and 'her beautiful son' lay in state at Lower Lodge
for twenty-four hours before the funeral. Two of the Royal
Dukes, York and Clarence, walked with Leopold. The Prince
Regent said he was too grief-stricken and stayed at home at
Carlton House. The *Morning Chronicle* wrote:

> 'History does not afford us an instance of such unequivocal
> heartfelt and universal tribute to the shade of any Prince or
> Potentate. Every patriot heart rejoiced in the prospect that a
> Princess so amiable was next in succession to the Prince Regent
> of the Realm . . .'

B [33]

The funeral was marred by scuffles and rioting which broke out when the officers at the doors of the Royal Chapels tried to cash in on the event by making people pay to enter. Nevertheless the nation was able to congratulate itself on its impressive show of moneyed grief: 'We never saw such a great concourse of well-dressed individuals,' wrote one newspaper. 'But the scene was not alone an exemplar of the superior wealth, but of the superior sensibility and moral pre-eminence of the British people.'

When Charlotte's father died as King thirteen years later there were no signs of feeling, no sorrow, no joy – 'only a bustle in the streets'. (It was not until nearly a century later that the whole nation again mourned wholeheartedly.)

The 90th and the 39th psalms were sung. The organ played *Dead March in Saul* and Charlotte's coffin, with melancholy solemnity, was lowered into the mouth of the vault built by her grandfather, George III. The inscription in 'modern Latinity' did not mention her mother's name so as not to offend her father. Her companion corpses were her aunt, Princess Amelia, and her maternal grandmother and great-aunt, the Duchess of Brunswick.

★   ★   ★

III

Grief and the Brighton
Secret Passage

Christmas/New Year 1817–18

Even Napoleon in St Helena was dismayed by Princess Charlotte's death. He said it was amazing that the English did not line up all their doctors and stone them. Lord Byron in Venice penning the fourth canto of *Childe Harold* wrote: 'The death of the Princess Charlotte has been a shock even here and must have been an earthquake at home.' Into *Childe Harold* he inserted: 'In the dust, the fair-haired daughter of the Isles is laid, The love of millions, how we did intrust Futurity to her. . . .' These lines well summed up how the people loved her and how their hopes for the succession were destroyed. Manufacturers cashed in on the grief: commemorative pictures and engravings, medals and china of Charlotte flooded the market, together with memorial books, pamphlets and poems. The mourning went from the sublime to the ridiculous; an anagrammatist wrote in the *Morning Chronicle*: 'Princess Charlotte Augusta of Wales may be transposed as follows, omitting the letters "PC" which as they stand for "Princess Charlotte" may with propriety be placed at the head thus:-

P.C.
HER AUGUST RACE IS LOST
O! FATAL NEWS.'

The epitaphs that were published in the popular press emphas-

[35]

ised that she had been England's one hope among the spend-thrift, loose-living Brunswicks:

> 'Mourn, Britain's Prince, thine only child is flown,
> The fairest brilliant that adorned thy crown.
> Born to rekindle virtue's dwindling blaze
> From pure Morality's neglected rays . . .'

The nation would have sacrificed all others in the Royal Family to save Charlotte. But just before Christmas John Croker, Secretary of the Admiralty, wrote to Sir Robert Peel: 'Our grief, as you must see, is wearing off, and the public is in, I think, rather a sulky humour, waiting for any fair or unfair excuse to fly into a passion. . . . If there should arise any division in the Royal Family, it will be the match to fire the gunpowder.'

Suspicion and anger were everywhere. What *had* happened at Claremont? Was Charlotte poisoned? Why was she starved for the fifty hours of her labour? Why hadn't the Prince Regent attended the funeral? Guilt? Why had Croft kept her short of food? Why had he allowed her to be weakened by anaemia? Why had he bled her so much? Had Leopold been drugged to keep him away from the scene of death? Why wasn't Mr Sims allowed into her room? Croft was accused of ignorance, mis-management and neglect. Dr Baillie was said to have 'expressed his doubts with regard to the event'.

The *Morning Chronicle* reflected the growing concern:

> 'It will scarcely be credited that there was not one lady, or even female domestic, resident at Claremont, whose experience could authorise her to be useful to the Princess during her pregnancy, or labour. Not one of them was a mother.
>
> 'Strange also . . . only one accoucheur present . . . Dr Sims did not assist in the delivery . . . The small quantity of serum found on the pericardium did not account for the death . . . of a labour so lingering . . . It is lamentable that the confinement of a Princess . . . should be at such a distance. Surely the paternal roof, or Buckingham House, or some other suitable mansion in town might have been assigned to the Princess . . . Preparations

were not made with sufficient regard to the importance of the case . . .'

Other criticisms followed. Why had the Queen been 108 miles away at Bath? Why had not one relative been present at the birth? Why had the Prince Regent gone away on 27 October with his mistress to a shoot over 100 miles away? The questions rang around the world. Something had been attempted or imprudently neglected. Charlotte's death was a scandal. Had one of her ambitious uncles or even her father made an arrangement with Croft? Newspapers called for an investigation into the doctor's mode of treatment.

Two days after the death, the Prince Regent's aide wrote a letter to Croft exonerating him of blame:

'Sir B. Bloomfield is honoured by the commands of the Prince Regent to convey to Sir Richard Croft his Royal Highness's acknowledgements of the zealous care and indefatigable attention manisfested towards his beloved daughter, during her late eventful confinement, and to express HRH's entire confidence in the medical skill and ability which he displayed during the arduous and protracted labour . . .'

The letter was published in newspapers but it did not protect Croft from 'the most illiberal aspersions'.

Some writer came out in defence of Croft noting that almost the whole of the Royal Family were subject to violent spasms which were hereditary. Others said that Charlotte's death had been caused by her 'noble but unsafe resolution to repress her feelings'. And, just in case that was the cause of her post-natal death, women in labour up and down England yelled and screamed to save themselves from 'Charlotte's fate'.

Ministers now said that an official investigation was impossible as the Prince Regent had expressed his approbation and awarded his thanks. He alone had the power to open an enquiry. But how could the Regent have known what had happened when he had been over 100 miles away at Sudbourn Hall at the time?

Rumours spread that the Regent and the old Queen had arranged to have Charlotte poisoned because while Charlotte was alive the Regent could never dare divorce her mother. The only precedent for divorce by a monarch was that established by Henry VIII; the only grounds for such a divorce would be adultery. But adultery by a monarch's wife or the wife of the heir to the monarch meant death. If the Prince of Wales divorced Caroline she would have the same fate as the beheaded Ann Boleyn and Katherine Howard: death for adultery. But the public would not stand for their future Queen, Charlotte, to be motherless – like Elizabeth after her mother Ann Boleyn was beheaded to get her out of the way so Henry VIII could marry and get a son. What had the Regent done to pave the way for divorce? Whispers of strange violence, of murder, of intrigue and unmentionable crime and doubts continued. The *Courier* as a supporter of royalty, criticised 'those who were industriously throwing out the darkest insinuations'.

A medical attack was led by Jesse Foot in a letter to the *Sun* on 13 November, entitled 'On the necessity of a Public Inquiry into the Cause of the death of Princess Charlotte and her Infant'. Foot was a well-known surgeon who tried to surpass John Hunter in fame. His letter protested that the public could not remain satisfied with what they had from the newspapers and asked if it was really true that the doctors had gone to bed and left Charlotte with the nurse. Gossip and much talk continued at all levels.

After the funeral, which he did not attend, the Regent escaped the public glare by retreating to the pleasures and peculiarities of his own original creation, Brighton, accompanied by his current mistress, the Marchioness of Hertford, a rotation of house guests, his aide Sir Benjamin Bloomfield and Lady Bloomfield.

It was at this time that the Regent not only granted Bloomfield a pension of £1200 a year, but named him Envoy and Minister Plenipotentiary in Sweden, at £9000 a year, and made him a Colonel of artillery at £1000 a year. Enemies suggested that the salary increase was a reward for arranging for the disposal of Princess Charlotte. But his sudden reward was more likely because he deftly suppressed a scandal over some jewels which had been given by the Regent to his mistress. They turned out to be part of the Crown Jewels. Lord Bloomfield, as he became, owed his elevation to the Peerage to his musical talents and tact. When the Prince of Wales was first living at the Pavilion, he wanted a man who could accompany him on the violincello, and having ascertained that Captain Bloomfield of the Royal Artillery, who was then at Brighton with his troop, was an accomplished violincello player, the captain was summoned to appear before the Prince. Their first meeting started an intimacy which lasted for many years. The musical soldier became the musical Prince's equerry.

But over Christmas/New Year, 1817/1818, at the Oriental pleasure-house in Brighton with its bathrooms with hot and cold running water and the newly introduced gas lighting, the Prince Regent suffered a deeper than deep depression. He described it to his mother as a 'sort of mishmash, Solomongrundy Olla podrida kind of business in itself . . .' His ill-health made his aides uneasy. The scandals that had reached him from Italy respecting the Princess of Wales increased his gloom and irritation.

Gossips joked that the Pavilion had become hell. The heat of the Pavilion was a constant source of complaint among the Prince's guests. He disliked cold intensely, and had a 'sort of patent stove' placed in the hall to heat the building – which it did so effectively that his guests were nearly suffocated. The room in which the Prince dined was known among them as 'the Royal oven'. It had a domed ceiling, and all air was excluded and when a fire was lit there, together with the 'patent stove' in the hallway, the diners roasted. A wit was dining one day inside this 'Royal oven' when he said to a friend: 'How do you feel yourself?' 'Hot,' gasped his friend, 'hot as hell.' 'It is quite right,' was the reply, 'that all of us here should be prepared in this world for what we may be sure will be our climate in the next.'

Both the Marchioness of Hertford and the gouty, rheumatic Regent looked as if they would soon be testing the climate in the next world. The Marchioness was attempting to hide the irreparable outrages of time, by never appearing at the Pavilion, except by artificial light. She had a separate house connected to the

Pavilion by a covered way. The Prince rose at three in the afternoon.

The Pavilion was sombre and sad and, as the court was in
mourning, balls or concerts were impossible. The Prince, however, had a band of musicians playing horns and other brass
instruments in the vestibule beside the patent stove, from dinner
until the Prince went to bed. He was delighted by the booming
band and beat time to it with the dinner gong.

The Regent's rest in Brighton with his Marchioness was com-
plicated by the presence of his legitimate but illegal wife, Mrs
Fitzherbert, who now received an allowance but no friendship
from the Prince. He didn't speak to her. Their union had produced no children, but it had in effect produced the town of
Brighton. Although they had separated five years earlier, Mrs
Fitzherbert had made this new resort her home.

Her presence in Brighton is described in Croker's journal:

'One reason why Mrs F. may like this place is that she is
treated as queen, at least of Brighton. They don't quite Highness her in her domestic circle, but they Madam her prodigi-
ously, and stand up longer for her arrival than for ordinary
folks, and in short, go as near to acknowledging her for
Princess as they can, without actually giving her the title. When
she dines out she expects to be led out to dinner before peeresses
– mighty foolish all this! The Duke of York still keeps up a
correspondence with her . . .'

When she went to Paris the French regarded her as the mor-
ganatic wife of the Regent and she was well received by the
French Royal Family. She was never received officially by the
King or Queen in England.

In 1817, she and her adopted daughter, Mary Seymour, were
staying in Brighton for Christmas and New Year, in the Steine
House the Regent had built her after their first reconciliation in
1803.

The mansion was large, airy and comfortable. A wide, covered
verandah, running the whole length of the front, was the centre
of the house. Mrs Fitzherbert served 'dishes of tea' to her friends

here. She watched the scene: all Brighton walked, rode or drove on the Steine in those days and auctions, sporting carnivals, militia drilling, betting rings in races week, Punch and Judy shows and military band concerts took place. In the years they had been together, the Prince of Wales had often been seen on Mrs Fitzherbert's verandah, especially in the morning. They sat idly looking at the sea and entertainments and talking for hours. Sometimes if he saw an acquaintance below he would smile or bow.

But, although seen on Mrs Fitzherbert's verandah, the Prince had seldom been seen entering or leaving the house. He loved mystery, and it was rumoured that a secret underground passage ran between the oriental pleasure palace and Mrs Fitzherbert's house. The Prince liked underground tunnels and had an underground passage dug leading from his private apartments at the Pavilion – near the large sunken bath filled with heated piped sea water – to his stables and the Dome.

Over Christmas and New Year, 1818, the Regent continued in low spirits and in low health. The usual gaieties of the Pavilion were suspended because of mourning for Princess Charlotte, but outside in the town reviews, naval displays, races, cricket matches, boating and donkey rides still continued.

The Regent looked dreadful – he left off his corsets, and according to Creevey 'his stomach dropped to his knees'. Cobbett estimated that he weighed 'perhaps a quarter of a ton'. He did not go out much. It was said this was because of guilt, but Croker attributes his secluded life at this time to avoiding the embarrassment of an encounter with Mrs Fitzherbert. Croker wrote:

'I cannot but wonder at her living here and bearding the Prince in a way so indelicate, vis-à-vis the public, and, I should have thought, so embarrassing to herself. To her presence is attributed the Prince's never going abroad at Brighton. I have known HRH here seven or eight years, and never saw or heard of his being on foot out of the limits of the Pavilion, and in general he avoids even riding through the principal streets. I cannot see how poor old Mrs Fitzherbert . . . can cause him any uneasiness . . .'

Whether the Prince of Wales's uneasiness that winter was caused by Mrs Fitzherbert, or by the circumstances of his daughter's death, no one could say. But then the Prince always liked intrigue – and kept mysteries bigger than his blocked-up secret tunnels.

The Prince of Wales had been acting as Regent since 1811. His father, George III, had sat on the throne to address the House of Commons and began: 'My Lords and Peacocks . . .' He never addressed Parliament again. For years he had been violent, often incoherent, and ill with agitation and 'hurry'. From the time of the death of Princess Amelia in 1810 he had been insane.

It had been during George III's fit of lunacy in 1788/9 that the word 'potty' became a slang word for 'mad'. A pamphlet *History of the Royal Malady by a Page of the Presence*, published in 1789 by Phillip Withers describes a scene in the locked room where the mad King was a prisoner. The pamphlet is a collection of anecdotes of the Royal Family and although some of them are true others are exaggerated and invented. Withers relates that the King was sitting in an armchair swaddled in fine linen like an Egyptian mummy as it was before straitwaist jackets were used to control him during his violent fits . . .

'Sir George (Baker) came in and unfastened his (the King's) arms to feel his pulse; whereupon the Royal patient gave him a blow on the forehead which laid him on the floor, and then poured over him the contents of the chamber pot. Standing over his physician, and reciting the rules of the "Order of Cloacina" (Cloacina was the Goddess of Privies, a subject of much lavatory humour), His Majesty exhorted Sir George to maintain its honour and dignity. He then retired to his chair and said, "Rise, Sir George, Knight of the most ancient, most puissant, and most honourable Order of Cloacina". After which he laughed himself to sleep. . . .'

One of the most persistent legends about the King's madness also originates from this pamphlet: in 1788, so the story goes, the King got out of his coach in Windsor Great Park and shook hands with an oak tree which he mistook for Frederick the Great.

In 1818, locked away in the most castellated of Royal residences, the King lived austerely. His apartments in the lower suite over-looking North Terrace are described by a contemporary:

'The King occupied three compartments, two of which formed one sitting-room, having an arched open communic-ation between bedroom and sitting-room and a large apartment of the suite which was allotted to his personal attendants. All these rooms contained furniture of the most homely descrip-tion ... HM's bed stands in a little recess and is hardly larger or more luxurious than the commonest kind of officer's camp bed. There is only a simple mattress, one bolster and no pillow ...'

With his father invisible, the Prince of Wales became monarch in every way except in name. In his elegant silks and satins, he had come to be wholeheartedly hated by his father's subjects. His collector's greed in furniture, pictures, silver, horses, clothes and jewels disgusted the 'nation of shop-keepers' and infuriated the hungry. His gambling, his vindictiveness towards his wife, his cruelty to Charlotte, his many mistresses and his astronomical debts were scandalous. He was hissed at and spat at wherever he went. His mistress, Lady Hertford, had to be rescued by Bow Street Runners when an immense mob seized her sedan chair and tried to overturn it.

When the Prince had opened Parliament on 28 January 1817, reformers presented petitions with half a million signatures. He condemned 'those exciting a spirit of sedition and violence'. Out-side, a silent crowd was waiting: they hissed the Regent in his carriage surrounded by Life Guards as he drove up the Mall. Stones flew, and two bullets shattered the carriage windows.

Committees investigating the assassination attempt found clear evidence of a revolutionary movement in London and in the new factory slums of Lancashire, Leicestershire, Derby, Nottingham and Glasgow. There were repeated riots and demonstrations in both agricultural and industrial districts, caused by heavy un-employment, pitiful wages, long hours, appalling conditions and the exploitation of child labour. Six-year-old children were disciplined by strappers in factories. Some of the protesters, undernourished on a workers' diet of bread, potatoes and tea, appealed to the government by yoking themselves to loaded wagons which they drew, like horses, from town to town. Demonstration was their only outlet as they had no vote.

A month later, in February, a nervous Parliament suspended Habeas Corpus, so that anyone under suspicion could be thrown into prison without trial, and passed further restrictive acts, including the prohibition of seditious meetings. Spies were employed to prowl among the restive, starving workers. Demonstrations and marches were dispersed by the yeomanry and regular troops. Their ring-leaders were sent to Australia – or to the gallows. Convict ships disposed of undesirables and returned to England with exotic plants, cages of kangaroos, parrots and wallabies – the latest diversions for the eccentric grandees.

The Prince Regent's brother, the Duke of Cambridge, wrote that 'nothing but firmness' could quell 'the abominable revolutionary spirit now prevalent in England'. In radical circles, the conviction was growing that the change from a monarchy to a republic was only a matter of time. The French Revolution had occurred just over twenty years ago and its memory was fresh. Even those who loved the Crown, such as the Duke of Bedford, confessed that they did not see how it could survive.

Charlotte's death in November had removed the only cherished member of the 'glorious House of Hanover' and headed it towards extinction. George III's family was the largest in the history of European royalty, but, it seemed, one of the most fruitless. His twelve living children, now all over forty, had produced a rumoured fifty-six bastards but only one legitimate heir to ensure the continuity of the dynasty. Now she was dead, each of the twelve brothers and sisters would have a chance to sit on the throne before lying in a coffin. England would have a series of geriatric and erratic monarchs; the crown would adorn the bald pates or grey heads of seven childless brothers, then the silver hairs of the five childless sisters, before passing to 'Silly Billy' Gloucester and to the thirteen-year-old Duke of Brunswick, a half-wit German nephew of George III.

The situation was summarised in a list published by the Press of 'the descendants now living of the Electress Sophia (grand-daughter of James I) to whose issue, being Protestants, the succession is limited: –

'*1. Descendants of George III, Eldest Son of Frederick, Prince of Wales, who was Great Grandson of the Electress Sophia.*

	Age
1. George, Prince of Wales, Prince Regent, Son*	55
2. Frederick, Duke of York, Son*	54
3. William, Duke of Clarence, Son	52
4. Edward, Duke of Kent, Son*	50
5. Ernest, Duke of Cumberland, Son*	46
6. Augustus, Duke of Sussex, Son	44
7. Adolphus, Duke of Cambridge, Son	43
8. Charlotte, Queen of Wurtemberg, Daughter.	51
9. Augusta of England, Daughter	49
10. Elizabeth of England, Daughter	48
11. Mary of England, Duchess of Gloucester*	41
12. Sophia of England, Daughter.	40

'*2. Descendants of William, Henry of Gloucester, Younger Son of Frederick, Prince of Wales*

13. William, Duke of Gloucester, Son	41
14. Sophia of Gloucester, Daughter	44

'*Descendants of Augusta of England, Duchess of Brunswick, elder daughter of Frederick, Prince of Wales (she died 1813)*

15. Charles, Duke of Brunswick, Grandson	13
16. William of Brunswick, Grandson	12
17. Augustus of Brunswick, Son	48
18. Frederick, King of Wurtemberg, Grandson*	36'

(*= married)

The list stops at the first heir who was married *with* children – the eighteenth in succession. Instead of a vertical succession (going as usual from father to son to grandson), the crown would slide sideways and be inherited horizontally.

The prospect was disturbing, and given the unsettled political situation it could be disastrous. The *Leeds Intelligencer*, a prominent provincial paper, wrote:

'Under the despondency which oppresses us, we look around with gloomy forebodings, with few hopes, many fears, with nearly a dread of certainty of evil, on all sides. We may in not many years see the Crown of England placed on twelve different heads – a prospect embarrassing, alarming and dangerous . . . a succeeding foreign prince, with foreign manners, might encroach upon our liberties . . .'

The result, it concluded, might be civil war. The British did not want another monarch out of the German nobility, the 'Sour Kraut' or 'German Sausages' of popular satire.

The American press regarded the possibilities wryly. 'The three persons nearest the throne, being married and having children, are the King of Wirtumbergh [*sic*], Prince Paul his brother and the Princess Frederica Bonaparte, the wife of Jerome Bonaparte!' (Napoleon's youngest brother) reported the *Vermont Northern Seninel*. 'How mortifying would it be to John Bull to see the Bonaparte blood on the British throne, to destroy which he has lavished oceans of blood and millions of treasure.' William Hone published four editions of a pamphlet 'with clear statements showing the succession to the crown, and the probability of the wife of Jerome Bonaparte becoming Queen and her son Jerome Napoleon, being Prince of Wales, and afterwards King of These Realms'.

Repugnance at the thought of a foreign King vied with reluctance to envisage a rapid succession of reigns in England – Frederick I, William IV, Edward VII, Ernest I &c. One newspaper predicted 'that in the next twenty-two years there will be nine reigns, two of them female; and that after the first there will be no reign longer than twenty-one months, and two as short as five months'.

'People try to amuse themselves,' wrote Lady Cowper, 'and their imaginations see a long train of crowns like Macbeth's passing before them.'

In this dangerous, uncertain atmosphere one thing was imperative; someone must beget an heir. A direct, legitimate and Protestant heir was required for the national peace of mind and perhaps for the survival of the monarchy itself.

The appropriate and natural man to get an heir was the Regent himself; but first, he must get a divorce. The behaviour of his wife, who had left England in 1814, was providing some hopes for this. She was travelling around Europe and the Near East with Bergami (whom she had elevated from Signor to Baron), and sleeping with him though he was thirty-two and she was an overblown fifty. Followed by her 200 courtiers and parasites, she had ridden into Jerusalem on an ass and set up the Order of St Caroline of Jerusalem, with Bergami as Grand Master and her adopted son William Austin – alleged to be her illegitimate child in the 'Delicate Investigation' – as its most honoured knight. Reports of this and countless other absurdities were reaching England at the time of Charlotte's death, and the Regent's main law officer, Sir John Leach, was drawing up a plan of procedure towards a divorce. But a great deal of weighty evidence was needed and proceedings would inevitably be slow.

So the main burden of Royal reproduction fell upon the Royal Dukes. What function did they serve, after all, if not to maintain the dynasty? They must each seek the hand of a nubile female of excellent Royal Protestant stock and get her pregnant as soon as could be arranged.

A matrimonial panic started. The Royal bulls rushed off proposals, each racing to grab the financial rewards granted to those who married for the dynasty. Germany, well stocked in Protestant Royalty was the obvious field of play. 'It will not excite surprise, if four nuptial ceremonies and one divorce enliven Old England,' wrote the *Ghent Journal*. 'Nothing is talked but marriages, divorces and posterity,' commented Lady Cowper in London. 'The competitors are in great spirits.'

A national tragedy had turned into a strange kind of national sporting event. The ever-ready satirist, Peter Pindar, turned out a sixty-page booklet entitled:

HUNTING FOR THE HEIR
THE ROYAL HUMBUGS or LUMPS OF LOVE

'Yoics! The Royal Sport's begun
I'faith but it is glorious fun
For hot and hard each Royal pair
Are at it hunting for the heir
Who gets the Heir the Crown shall win
The Commons are the shippers in.
Where's wide-mouth Sussex, give tongue Kent,
Sure they're for Heir-hunting a-bent.
. . . that worthy beagle Kent
To couple soon is his intent . . .'

*   *   *

IV
The Royal Marriages Act

The succession crisis of 1817/18 had come about because George III wanted to safeguard his family's Royal blood. George III had come to the throne when his grandfather, George II, died in the lavatory at Kensington Palace. Horace Walpole relates the story of George II's death:

> 'A little after seven he went into the water-closet; the German valet de chambre heard a noise, listened, heard something like a groan, ran in, and found the hero of Oudernarde and Dettingen on the floor, with a gash in his right temple, by falling against the corner of a bureau. He tried to speak, could not, and expired.'

George II's eldest son and heir, Frederick, had died nine years earlier after being hit by a tennis ball, so the King's youthful grandson, George, came to the throne at the age of twenty-two. Once installed as monarch, the third George became pious. His first proclamation as sovereign in 1760 had prohibited dice, cards and other games in public or private on Sundays. He announced his determination 'to discountenance and punish all manner of vice, profaneness and immorality, in all persons of whatsoever degree or quality . . . and particularly in such as are employed near our Royal person . . .' The sexual mores of his two brothers and his sister were to his mind distinctly unregal, and this contributed to tormenting headaches, the frequent pain of which had once caused him to have his hair cut off.

The need to protect the throne from any child conceived from mere lust, sexual relief or pleasure became urgent. George's youngest brother, the twenty-five-year-old Duke of Cumberland –a vain, idle and stupid sybarite – loved pretty Lady Grosvenor. After he seduced her, her husband sued the Duke for 'criminal conversation' (an eighteenth-century euphemism for adultery) and during the famous trial in March 1770, the Royal love letters were read in court. Phrases like: 'I dreamt of you . . . had you on the couch 10,000 times . . .' amused England. The Duke paid £10,000 damages – which he had to borrow – to the Earl, who left his wife. The wife of a timber merchant took Lady Grosvenor's place – until a note was shown by the Duke to the King reporting his marriage to Mrs Anne Horton, a notorious flirt and a widow. Mrs Horton had 'the most amorous eyes in the world' and a shady background; daughter of a parvenu peer, it was gossiped that after a conversation with her one felt like washing out one's ears. She was unacceptable to Royalty, so the King ostracised the newly-married Cumberlands and gave instructions to his Chamberlain that anyone who called on the Duke and Duchess in Cumberland House would not be received by the King or his wife, Queen Charlotte.

The next marital calamity was adultery by the King's sister, Caroline Matilda. After her marriage at the age of fifteen to the King of Denmark – whose sport was pursuing 'low amours' – Caroline Matilda became the lover of the Danish Prime Minister, Struensee, formerly a handsome young physician. Struensee was arrested, charged with adultery and hanged at the gallows: and the Queen was thrown into a cell at Croenenberg. In January 1772, she was taken to a tower in the castle of Zell, where she died three years later.

The King was determined that his favourite brother, the twenty-year-old Duke of Gloucester, would not marry the widow Lady Waldegrave with whom he lived. She too was unacceptable as she was the illegitimate offspring of Sir Edward Walpole's affair with a milliner.

This tendency of Princes of the Blood to mix with plebeian stock so disturbed the King that, at his personal instigation, the

Royal Marriages Bill was introduced to Parliament. It would make the marriages of the Royal Family a matter of State rather than of private desires. He and his wife Queen Charlotte ranked the pettiest Prince of Germany above the noblest of England's Dukes.

On 17 February 1772 a Bill was brought into Parliament entitled: 'An Act for the Better Regulating of the Future Marriages of the Royal Family'. The Bill was strongly opposed at all stages as despotic and un-English. Lord Chatham complained that it gave 'wanton and tyrannical' powers to the King.

The King wrote to his Prime Minister, Lord North:

'I do expect every nerve be strained to carry through both Houses with a becoming firmness, for it is not a question that immediately relates to Administration, but personally to myself; therefore I have a right to expect a hearty support from everyone in my service, and shall remember defaulters.'

Although Charles James Fox resigned from the government to attack the Bill, it was forced through. When it received the Royal Assent in March 1772, the King was happy: never again would a member of his family marry a plebeian. Never again would the Hanoverian blood be polluted with ordinary common stock; it would always be thick and blue.

Intended to guarantee the continued purity of the superior caste of Royalty and the dignity of the British monarch, the Act made any marriage of a descendant of George II null and void if he married without the Sovereign's consent. Princesses who married into foreign Royal families were exempt. If the Sovereign refused consent any Royalty over twenty-five could give a year's notice to the Privy Council and marry if Parliament made no objection.

There was much opposition to the Bill, both in Parliament and outside. It was criticised for being inhuman, an infringement of human rights, the embodiment of 'German pride' ('The daughters of our noble families . . . being at present thought only good enough for their whores but not for their wives,' wrote the *Evening News*); but, most of all – in Lord Holland's words when he tried to get the Act repealed in 1820 – as 'a law hostile to morality'.

The Act also threatened any person assisting in any marriage ceremony or contract with a descendant of George II who had not had Royal consent, with the Penalties of Praemunire – a punishment involving 'a total forfeiture of all goods and estates, imprisonment at the will of the King, and not to be relieved, even if starving'.

The King defended his action by saying that the Wars of the Roses were caused by marriages with the nobility. He wrote to the Duke of Gloucester:

'In any country a Prince marrying a subject is looked upon as dishonourable; nay in Germany the children of such a marriage cannot succeed to any territories; but here, where the Crown is but too little respected, it must be big with the greatest mischiefs. Civil wars would by such measures be again coming in this country, those of the Yorks and Lancasters were greatly owing to intermarriages with the nobility . . . I have children who must know what they have to expect if they could follow so infamous an example.'

Protected by the Act, the King thought he would now only have Princesses as sisters-in-law – but instead, he found he was brother-in-law to a bastard. Six months after the passing of the Bill, the King received a 'disagreeable' letter from his same favourite brother, Gloucester, revealing that he had been secretly married to Lady Waldegrave for six years, and she was now pregnant.

George III's eldest son always boasted that he would repeal his father's Royal Marriages Act when he came to power. He failed to do so because he had the problem of his own secret marriage. The Fitzherbert/Prince of Wales wedding certificate, now in the Royal Archives, would have made it impossible for the Prince to succeed if it had been valid as she was a Roman Catholic; and it was only irregular because of the unpopular Royal Marriages Act.

The position remains the same today with the Act of Settlement and the Royal Marriages Act. If Prince Charles were to marry without the Queen's permission not only would the marriage be null and void and any issue illegitimate, but the clergyman or registrar could have all his possessions confiscated and be thrown into prison. (The Act still covers all descendants of George II. The public were reminded of this when Lord Harewood – a second cousin of the Queen – had to obtain the Queen's permission when he remarried after a divorce.)

It was thought that the Royal Marriages Act would be short-lived, a measure that would be repealed or fall into disuse on the death of George III. Yet 205 years later it is still in force. Each Sovereign has had despotic power to forbid the marriages of his sons, daughters and relatives. In its 205 years of existence, no appeal to Parliament against the Sovereign's decision has been made by any Prince or Princess of the blood.

After his father went totally mad in 1810 and he assumed power in 1811, the Prince Regent enforced the Royal Marriages Act with paternalistic severity and made it difficult for his brothers and sisters to marry whom they wanted.

Once in power, the Regent – like his father – had an exalted idea of the monarchy and the superior caste of Royalty. English women could only be repositories for Royal sperm, not mothers of kings.

In the *Public Advertiser*, one satirist wrote: 'Such an Act will tend to the Encouragement of Fornication and Adultery, to the great Detriment of His Majesty's loyal Subjects, unless some Methods are taken to lessen the amorous Dispositions and Vigour of the Royal Heirs . . .' Sir Joseph Mawbey moved a correction to the title of the Act. It should read: 'An Act for Enlarging and Extending the Prerogative of the Crown, and for the Encourage-ment of Adultery and Fornication under the Pretence of Regu-lating the Marriages of the Royal Family.'

When someone once criticised a Royal Duke for keeping a mistress in Kensington Palace, Princess Charlotte retorted: 'Oh, Lord upon us. What would you have? The Dukes cannot marry, they must love somebody.'

The Regent's brothers and sisters – even when over forty – could wed none but approved Protestant Royalty (German,

Dutch or Danish). Germany at least was a sturdy purveyor of brides and bridegrooms for after the Napoleonic Wars in 1815 there were thirty-nine separate states in Germany and thirty-nine separate 'Royal' families. But the domains of many a German Prince were not as large as the estate of an English country gentleman.

One visitor, guilty of a misdemeanour in the territory of one of these numerous German Princes, was ordered to quit His Serene Highness's dominions within twenty-four hours. He replied he could do so in ten minutes: he only had to walk a few paces to the right or to the left.

Originally the states of Germany, dating from the time of Charlemagne, had at different times, according to the German custom, set aside portions of land specifically to provide for younger sons. Divisions therefore had been followed by continual sub-divisions. Etiquette and ceremony were kept up at the courts of these petty German Sovereigns to a degree laughable to an English Duke. Nearly each of the thirty-nine Princes had his Prime Minister, Minister for War, Great Chamberlain, Marshal and all the trappings and pomp of Royalty. The Duke of Hesse's magnificent carriage was accompanied by footmen in lavish liveries, running by the side with torches.

The Royal Marriages Act made these small German courts, with their exaggerated ceremonies, the hatcheries for the British Royal Family. The aristocracy in England was *not* a closed caste as on the continent; English farmers, soldiers, MPs were frequently transformed from plain Esquires into 'Lords', 'Earls', and 'Viscounts'. If it had not been for the Royal Marriages Act the English monarchy might easily have gone the same way as the aristocracy. To continentals an English Lord was a joke. But George III ensured that his Royal Family conformed to rigid continental dynastic practices – and would continue to do so – despite the advance of the vote and democratic ideas.

George III not only created the Royal Marriages Act; he made the most of Royal Marriage – he and his wife, Queen Charlotte, had fifteen children of whom thirteen survived to adulthood and twelve survived into wrinkled old age and did not die until their

late fifties, sixties and seventies. They were the largest adult
Royal Family in the history of European monarchy. Edward III
had been the last English monarch to have a family of adult
Princes and he had had only five sons. With twelve children over
forty the House of Hanover seemed to be in very good hands.
But it was not. It was as if George III's children were revolting
against this attempt to impose a system of eugenics on the Royal
Family. The Royal Marriages Act discouraged Royal breeding
and the Prince of Wales became the Act's greatest victim.

★   ★   ★

V

The Candidates

The Royal Marriages Act was much to blame for the predicament of the English Royal Family in November 1817. But Napoleon had also contributed to the unmarried state of George III's children. Between 1803 and 1813 he and his armies had kept Europe more or less out of bounds to them. So for much of their lives as eligible bachelors and spinsters they had been deprived of their natural matrimonial market: what were now the forty-nine states of Germany. With Napoleon a prisoner on St Helena only a ring of salt water stood between the Dukes and their prospective brides.

But the children of George III presented an altogether dismal picture at this time.

Of the King's twelve surviving offspring, only three were legally married (the Prince Regent was separated from Caroline and planning to divorce her), and these marriages were without offspring. At Windsor Castle the Queen, a severe matriarch, now so fat and distended by dropsy that she looked 'as if she was giving birth to all her fifteen children at once' kept a weary grip over three ageing spinster daughters known as 'the sisterhood' or 'the old girls'.

The eldest of these, Augusta, was now at forty-nine too old to hope for issue even if she could find a suitable husband. Her youthful beauty had been drowned in corpulence. Her love for her father's equerry, Sir Brent Spencer, had been thwarted by both the Royal Marriages Act and her mother's possessive jealousy. She was destined to spinsterhood for the rest of her quiet, unassuming life.

Her sister Sophia was nine years younger but weak and delicate, a lifelong prey to ill-health. She was as thin as Augusta was fat.

At twenty-three she had borne an illegitimate child to General Garth; it was also rumoured that she had had incestuous relations with her brother Ernest. But she had aged early and retreated into the security of the family.

The most talented and remarkable of the 'old girls' was Princess Elizabeth. Bright, witty, generous and imaginative, she had frequently found it cruelly depressing to remain thus under her mother's thumb, and had declared that she 'would marry as soon as ever she found an opportunity of doing so'. But the only offer had come from the penniless exiled Duke of Orleans and had been literally laughed out of court by the Royal Family. She was forty-seven, and her prospects were growing slimmer as she grew fatter.

As for the two daughters who had managed to escape, their marriages looked more like desperation than love. The Princess Royal, named Charlotte like her mother and niece, had at thirty-three captured the King of Wurtemberg. The marriage was fruitless. The only child she had conceived had been still-born. She had been the first of the daughters who had married and now, at fifty-one, was a widow and as short of breath and as obese as her late husband, who had had to have carpenters cut deep curves in tables and desks at his Stuttgart palace to accommodate his elephantine stomach. Her strange delight was to watch her pet kangaroos jumping.

Princess Mary had left what was referred to as 'The Nunnery, Windsor Castle' to marry her first cousin, the Duke of Gloucester, known – with good reason – as 'Silly Billy'. He was, according to Stockmar, 'large and stout, but with weak helpless legs . . . prominent meaningless eyes; without being actually ugly a very unpleasant face with an animal expression'. He was the only son of George III's late brother, the Duke of Gloucester, whose marriage to the illegitimate daughter of Sir Edward Walpole and a milliner had been a contributory factor to the introduction of the Royal Marriages Act. Even if he were capable of consummating marriage, there was nothing to show for it.

So the five daughters of the King, with an average age of forty-five, had failed to produce a single living legitimate child. His

seven sons had made an equally unimpressive performance. Three
of them were married within the terms of the Royal Marriages
Act. Of these, leaving aside the Prince Regent himself, the eldest
was fifty-four-old Frederick, Duke of York. Frederick expected
to seize power any day, as his father and brother were being
bled for illnesses and gout. His name was synonymous with scandal; in 1809 a House of Commons enquiry had exposed his mistress Mary Clarke for selling military commissions and promotions
like a broker while he was Commander-in-Chief of the Army.
He resigned.

Supporting his enormous girth on legs too weak for the task,
so that, according to Stockmar, 'one was always afraid he would
tumble over backwards', the 'Grand Old Duke of York' appeared
a slave to greed and lust. The famous nursery rhyme about his
'ten thousand men' – 'he marched them up to the top of the hill,
then he marched them down again' – was a popular jibe at his
military incompetence.

He had had twenty-five years of childless marriage to a Prussian
Princess. The Duchess of York now lived at Oatlands Park,
Weybridge; the Duke of York went home every weekend
accompanied by smart friends. Greville's description of life there
gives some idea of why Frederick was not the best placed man
to provide an heir to the throne:

'I went to Oatlands on Saturday. There was a very large
party . . . We played at whist till four in the morning. On
Sunday we amused ourselves with eating fruit in the garden,
and shooting at a mark with pistols, and playing with the
monkeys. I bathed in the cold bath in the grotto, which is as
clear as crystal and as cold as ice. Oatlands is the worst managed
establishment in England; there a great many servants, and
nobody waits on you; a vast number of horses, and none to
ride or drive . . .

'The parties at Oatlands take place every Saturday, and the
guests go away on Monday morning. These parties begin as
soon as the Duchess leaves London, and last till the October
meetings. During Egham races there is a large party . . . this is

the Duchess's party . . . We dine at eight and sit at table till eleven . . . The Duchess also plays at half-crown whist. The Duke always gets up very early, whatever time he may go to bed. On Sunday morning he goes to church, returns to a breakfast of tea and cold meat, and afterwards rides or walks till evening. On Monday morning he always sets off to London at nine o'clock. He sleeps equally in a bed or in a carriage.

'The Duchess seldom goes to bed, or, if she does, only for an hour or two; she sleeps dressed upon a couch, sometimes in one room sometimes in another. She frequently walks out very late at night, or rather early in the morning, and she always sleeps with open windows. She dresses and breakfasts at three o'clock, afterwards walks out with all her dogs, and seldom appears before dinner-time. At night, when she cannot sleep, she has women to read to her. The Duchess of York is clever and well-informed; she likes society and dislikes all form and ceremony, but in the midst of the most familiar intercourse she always preserves a certain dignity of manner . . . Her dogs are her greatest interest and amusement, and she has at least forty of various kinds. She is delighted when anybody gives her a dog, or a monkey, or a parrot, of all of which she has a vast number; it is impossible to offend her or annoy her more than by ill-using any of her dogs, and if she were to see anybody beat or kick any one of them she would never forgive it. She has always lived on good terms with the Royal Family, but is intimate with none of them, and goes as little as possible to Court. The Regent dislikes her, and she him.'

The Duchess reigned at Oatlands – even over the stables. No one, not even the Duke, could take out the horses without her permission – which she seldom gave. As the Duchess had indulged in dogs instead of lovers, there was never a question of divorce, even though the marriage was childless.

The other married son was fifth in succession: Ernest, Duke of Cumberland, said to be the most unpopular man in England. Stockmar describes him as 'a tall, powerful man, with a hideous face; can't see two inches before him; one eye turned quite out of its place'. He had married his cousin three years earlier after she had buried (murdered? the public asked) one husband, and divorced another, who later died. Princess Charlotte had commented on the match and the trouble it was causing her father who was 'in a bit of a scrape' as he had asked his ministers to 'make out a handsome allowance' for the Duke 'which they declared they would not venture to do . . . on account of the Duke's unpopularity, and the lady's notorious bad reputation, for it will at once revive and renew all the old stories about her . . .'

The Queen used the fact that Princess Frederica of Mecklenburg-Strelitz had married the 'Prince of Solms when she was engaged to the Duke of Cambridge, and many other circumstances of which I am more imperfectly apprized . . .' as an excuse why she could not receive her. So the Queen wrote to her son telling him '. . . I cannot but rejoice that She does not accompany You to England'.

The Queen's rejection of her new daughter-in-law was good ammunition for the Opposition and the Bill to increase the Duke of Cumberland's allowance had been rejected by one vote. He had always been unpopular as a ferocious reactionary, and in 1810, after he had covered his bedroom walls with mirrors on every side, the public decided that he had practised every sort of decadent vice. There had been rumours that he had sexually assaulted his sister Sophia. It was also believed that he had murdered his valet, Sellis, who had been found dead with his throat slit in Cumberland's suite.

Nevertheless, Cumberland remained the one brother whose married life was reasonably likely to prove fruitful.

His marriage, and the Duke and Duchess of York's peculiar arrangement, should have left four eligible bachelors in the family. But the obese and eccentric Augustus, Duke of Sussex, had compromised his chances by an illegal marriage to Lady Augusta Murray, the second daughter of the Earl of Dunmore, when in Rome for a chest cure in April 1793. The ceremony had been repeated the following December in St George's, Hanover Square. But in 1794, this became the first marriage to be declared void under the Royal Marriages Act of 1772. There were two children,

Augustus Frederick D'Este who was twenty-three, in 1817, and Augusta Emma who was nineteen. The Duke's life was strewn with debts, plagued by asthma, and harassed by importunities from his 'left-handed' wife for money and royal status. The marriage was a flop, and 'Goosey' and 'Gussie' now lived separately.

In 1817 the Duke was in love with his library at Kensington Palace, which was one of the finest in private hands in the country, and his causes: reform, abolition, emancipation, and God. He always wore a black skull-cap so he wouldn't catch a chill and took joy in the finches which flew around his parlour at Kensington Palace. He also took an interest in the twenty-seven-year-old daughter of the Earl of Arran, Lady Cecilia, who had married the fifty-six-year-old widower and city merchant Sir George Buggin a few years earlier. (After her husband's death in 1825, Lady Cecilia changed her name to her mother's maiden name, Underwood, because of the frequent jokes about 'Buggin'.)

The Duke of Sussex's wife was loudly indiscreet about her marriage. She was so anxious to become a Royal Duchess and make her two children an official Prince and Princess that the Regent's equerries were in despair as to whether they had to invoke any of the penalty clauses under the Royal Marriages Act. Sir William Knighton wrote to the Prince Regent on 16 December 1817:

> 'I find it necessary, however, to keep my eye on the provincial papers . . . A journal at Leeds has lately been at work for the Duke of S[ussex]. They seem to have a crotchet and wish to legalise his son, whom they designate by the title of a fine spirited 'Prince'. They then notice that the Duke was married twice to the lady, and the last time at St George's Church, Hanover Square. All the papers relative to that affair are in your Royal Highness's possession, bearing great testimony . . .'

The Regent could not risk the Duke of Sussex remarrying in case it led to more enquiry about the Royal Marriages Act, which might make public his marriage to Mrs Fitzherbert. But the public was sympathetic about the limited scope of fecund wives. 'Would Englishmen be of the opinion that his Royal Highness's marrying an English woman was a good reason for depriving his issue of the crown? It is unsupposeable,' said one correspondent.

The most eligible of the four Royal bachelor Dukes was the gentle and careful forty-three-year-old Adolphus 'Dolly', Duke of Cambridge, the only son of George III who kept himself free of debt. He was Governor General of Hanover where he lived quietly if eccentrically, terrifying churchgoers by roaring answers to any rhetorical questions posed in sermons and shaking his pretty blond wig. (When the Ten Commandments were read out, he would amuse himself with remarking after 'Thou shalt not kill' – 'What! Not like my brother Cumberland!') In a family which talked with such rapidity that it was difficult often to follow, the Duke of Cambridge's excited sentences were outstanding.

Of all the unmarried sons it was imperative that the Duke of Cambridge should get a Duchess and make her pregnant. He was considered more likely to be fertile and potent than his other brothers, except for the Duke of Cumberland whose wife, whom he had married in 1815, was considered, at forty, too old for child-bearing. She had had a stillborn child the year previously, even though she had had sons by her previous two husbands.

The two remaining bachelor sons were so undesirable that though their brides might someday be Queens, they were not even considered eligible suitors by the eager spinster Princesses of Germany.

William, Duke of Clarence, fat and fifty-three, a constant user of obscene language, had been turned down by thirteen women. Father to ten bastards by his dead mistress, Dorothy Jordan (who had performed on the stage between confinements to subsidise his gambling debts), he now had debts of £56,000 which made marriage an urgent necessity.

The Regent had once said that he doubted if anyone would marry William, who wiped his nose with the back of his forefinger and shook his fist at his coachman. After Canning brought him into notice by making him High Admiral – in Whitehall, not at sea – he distinguished himself by making ridiculous speeches. He made speeches opposing Wilberforce's attempt to abolish slavery and opposing adultery. He exhibited oddities and some thought there were indications of incipient insanity.

Edward, Duke of Kent, the fourth brother, was in some ways the most repulsive of all. He was a large, powerful man with a head as bald and shiny as an onion, ringed by a few remaining tufts of hair dyed black to match his side-whiskers. He was brushed, polished, clean and polite. He was popular for his radical views in politics. But whatever could be said about his brothers – immoral, extravagant, stupid – none of them was, like Kent, an utterly humourless, self-righteous prig. He considered himself definitely their superior and they for their part hated 'Simon Pure'. His face in portraits exudes unlimited pomposity and unshakeable conceit. In his Army career, his zest for discipline made him a cruel superior. At every post he held, he left in his wake the broken and beaten bodies of private soldiers whose offence might be no more than an untied boot-lace. He had to be retired twice from the Governorship of Gibraltar because this savagery rebounded against him; on the second occasion, his banning of all alcohol on the Rock had led to a mutiny.

He could not see that he was at fault. If, thanks to his completely blind extravagance, he was in debt to the tune of £200,000, it was pure bad luck and the nation ought to help him out (but since it didn't, he hid from his creditors in Brussels); if he was living in sin, at least his companion was Madame de St Laurent, a French lady of good breeding and not an actress like Clarence's woman. Their mutual arrangement had lasted twenty-seven years and, like everything else about Kent – except his lash-happy discipline – was calm, comfortable and discreet.

After the two married brothers and the four bachelors, the only other candidate who could produce an heir – if his obesity and gout had not, as rumoured, caused impotence – was the fifty-nine-year-old Prince Regent himself, provided he could divorce Caroline, who was causing scandal in Italy. He appointed a secret committee to investigate her reckless conduct abroad, and collect evidence against her. Her sexual adventures caused horror and concern for the reputation of the Royal Family. But at the same time it was feared that Caroline was baiting the Regent; if he started divorce proceedings against her, the Regent's many enemies in Parliament would bring up details of his past and present mistresses and also stir up the ashes of his secret marriage to Mrs Fitzherbert. Under the Act of Settlement his marriage to a Roman Catholic would deprive him of the throne. He would end up as plain George Guelph, bigamist, instead of George IV. Caroline was credited with saying: 'Well, I have only committed adultery with one man, and he was Mrs Fitzherbert's husband.' He was the only monarch since Henry VIII to have initiated a divorce, except for George I who divorced his wife and locked her in a castle for thirty-two years before being chosen to be King of England.

The Regent's equerries and staff fed material for his hatred of Caroline. A few weeks after the death of Charlotte a letter arrived from Sir William Knighton about papers given to Mr Leach to begin investigations: '. . . whether it be Como, or Naples, or Tunis, the same habits, the intentions, and conduct prevail, hence the evident usefulness of your Royal Highness's judicious suggestion, of a distinct narrative of her general conduct . . .'

Although the Royal Family had retired into mourning for Princess Charlotte, her mother, Princess Caroline, is reported to have continued her pursuit of pleasure with only the slightest of pauses, for grief did not show at first when the Princess was told of the death of her daughter; but, when informed officially of the death, she made such a fuss leeches were put on to her temples and head.

The Regent, who always vacillated about whom and what he wanted, knew one thing for certain: he wanted to be free 'of the vilest wretch on earth'. He also wanted to remarry and produce an heir. Lord Lauderdale said that the Regent was definitely contemplating another wife. Prince Alexander of Solms wrote to him suggesting a daughter of Victor Emmanuel, King of Sardinia, would be suitable as he was a great-grandson of Anne of Orleans, the grand-daughter of Charles I, and thus the Stuart claimant to the throne of England. Mr W. H. Fremantle told the Marquess of Buckingham, 'that they are trying to cook up a match for the King with a Princess of Tours and Taxis (I believe a sister of the Duchess of Cumberland) and a sister of the Princess Esterhazy. Metternich is at the bottom of it.'

Divorce might indeed bring down upon the Regent's head an avalanche of abuse and recrimination – and an investigation into his own past life. But the course was set. He and his brothers and sisters lined up for the Crown Stakes. Of the sisters, two were married and childless, two were secretly married and not childless, and one was unmarried and forty-seven. Augusta and Sophia were disqualified by age and infirmity respectively, the Princess Royal by widowhood, and Mary by a fruitless marriage, leaving only Elizabeth as an outside runner. Of the seven brothers, York's wife was married to her dogs, Sussex's eccentric concerns turned him elsewhere, and Cumberland was already married to the notorious Frederica.

So there were five serious contestants in the Royal marriage race who had an urgent need of spouses: Elizabeth, Cambridge, Clarence, Kent and the Regent. Every inbred inch of them offered a handicap of some sort. The Prime Minister was offering increased prize money. He wrote to the Prince Regent on 17 January 1818 that he suggested a larger grant go to Clarence, the first brother to set proposals before him, than to Kent, etc., whose proposals came later. But the victor's reward would not only be monetary – there was the prospect of a child who would be God's principal supporter, Fidei Defensor – and whose face would back every coin in the land.

★　　　★　　　★

VI
The Altar Stakes

Winter 1817–18

The Royal Race now started. One morning, in his rented house in Brussels, the fifty-one-year-old Duke of Kent was breakfasting with Madame de St Laurent when she fainted over the *Morning Chronicle* which had arrived – with many bills – in the Duke's mail from England.

The editorial had as good as ordered her departure:

'The order of the Succession to the Crown is now by her (that is, Charlotte's) death disturbed; and from the age of the Princes in the order of succession, and the state of the illustrious family, apprehensions will occur to every loyal mind. It will be the earnest prayer of the nation, than an early alliance of one of the unmarried Princes may forthwith be settled. There were some time ago rumours of the intended marriage of the truly amiable and excellent Duke of Kent with a Princess of the House of Saxe-Coburg, one of the sisters of Prince Leopold, and we have reason to believe there was foundation for the report. Their [*sic*] is no union which the nation would hail with more rapturous delight, and for the establishment of which they would be more prompt liberally to contribute.'

What 'Madame' had been fearing for some time now, as Kent's debts accumulated, was now plainly set out before her: the Duke must leave her to marry. Even before his flight from England a year earlier, Kent had been quietly weighing up the appeal of the Parliamentary grant that marriage would bring him as a means of lightening a burden of debt that had become chronic.

He had been a debtor since the age of twenty, when he had

first set himself up to live in princely style. Debts had followed him through his Army career in Quebec (where he had met 'Madame'), America, the West Indies and Gibraltar. After the recall from his disastrously brutal Governorship of Gibraltar in 1803 he had cultivated a life-style far beyond his purse. His favourite residence in England – Castle Hill at Ealing – is described as being kept speckless twenty-four hours a day by night-servants and day-servants, manservants and maidservants. Each of these in turn was kept immaculate, powdered and pomaded by a resident hairdresser, who also dyed the Duke's long whiskers and few remaining tufts of hair. Every conceivable delicacy and refinement adorned Castle Hill – artificial songbirds, musical clocks, corridors of coloured lights.

By 1807, the Duke's debts totalled over £200,000. At this point he arranged for half his annual income of £24,000 to be consigned to trustees solely to pay interest on this amount. But with Waterloo and the end of the wars, creditors started demanding the return of their capital. A pleading letter to the Prince Regent, requesting an increase in his grant, was curtly turned down. The Duke decided to hand over three-quarters of his allowance to appointed trustees who would face the creditors as best they might, while he went to live in Brussels on a mere £7000 a year. But still old habits died hard; the exiled debtor rented the largest house he could find, and a contemporary, Mr Pryce Gordon, describes the results:

'The Duke's taste for architecture, embellishing and adorning was well known, and no one was surprised when a host of carpenters were put into requisition; and in a few months the house was so altered and ornamented (and of course improved) that the young count (whose property it was), when invited to see what the Royal Duke had done, could hardly recognise his late abode. The extensive gardens next attracted his Royal Highness's attention, and were newly modelled and replanted with the choicest flowers and rarest shrubs which the kingdom could produce. The stables and remises were furnished with stalls and mangers and pavements and ventilators, according to the most approved plans in England; and his Royal Highness's stud became the admiration of the public.'

All his life the Duke was obsessed with finicky detail. It was this same obsession for perfection which had made him intolerable in the Army and wrecked his career at Gibraltar. The preservation of orderly, pleasant appearances was the supreme concern and aspiration of his life.

Of course, he did not see himself in this light. His own point of view comes through in the contemporary pamphlet *The Rival Princes* which quotes his protégé, Dr Glennie:

'He observed that the Duke's affection for his old French lady, whom, he lamented, he could not marry, was a proof of his steady disposition, and domestic good qualities, added to which he regularly went to church and was never *seen inebriated* – a habit he *always* endeavoured to check in those over whom he had any *influence*.'

He thought of himself as a paragon of virtue compared to his sinful brothers. For his public life, he had three secretaries who helped him keep up a voluminous correspondence – so voluminous that Government departments lived in dread of receiving his long, boring letters and, according to Stockmar, 'his name was never uttered without a sigh by the functionaries of every public office'.

At home, the Duke was a tiresome old busybody. Come money or debts, for him four houses were a necessity. He may have been deprived of a career in the Army, but he kept military discipline among his staff. Everything was run with parade-ground precision.

'Never be above attending to particulars, ay, and minute particulars,' was his advice to a young friend. 'What is a trifle? Nothing that has reference to our comfort, our independence or our peace.' Thus, the wolf at the door was kept at bay by trivia. Along with his nit-picking, he was pompous, facile and long-winded in speech, like all his family a lover of the sound of his own voice.

He gave rein to this indulgence at innumerable public meetings for philanthropic causes. The mainstay of British charities, his name was subscribed to the conversion of the Jews, the encouragement of artisans, the relief of the distressed, the instruction of infant heathens, the supply of trusses to ruptured persons, and the delivery of poor women in their own habitations, among a total of fifty-three worthy institutions. Every petition the Duke received would be forwarded by him, no matter how little influence he had in the matter. His principles were, in fact, more likeable than his personality, for he was in public matters a sympathiser with progressive ideas, concerned with remedies for 'the evil of a depressed working class'.

But moral passion was not his strong point at home. He cared for comfort; he cared for his 'old French lady'; but it was evident that sooner or later the one must be sacrificed to the other. In 1816 Prince Leopold had suggested that Kent try for the hand of his sister Victoire. So, between leaving London and settling in Brussels, Kent had been on a short tour of Germany to take a look at her and at another possible cure for his insolvency, Princess Catherine of Baden, sister of the Tsarina; the latter, however, was so ugly as to make the profitable hypocrisy not worth it. He proposed to Victoire. She, though on most occasions ready to obligingly conform to all the roles expected of dutiful Princesses, could find little enthusiasm for this fat, bald, unprepossessing fifty-year-old bore, and refused. Her brother, anxious to strengthen the ties between his family and the Royal Family of England, pressed her to reconsider, and acted as a go-between, bringing her round to the now equally uncertain Duke.

The Duke of Kent was finding it an increasing strain thus to go behind the back of his mistress and oldest companion – 'the subject (of marriage) is frequently reverted to and occasions infinitely uncomfortable moments to us both', he told a friend. 'I had *always* flattered myself that, if such a circumstance took place, Mme de St L—— would have accepted an annual allowance from me, and tho' at a distance have maintained a habit of amicable intercourse by *letter*, which would have made me feel *comfortable* about her, after the agony of parting was once passed;

but all that she has stated to me of her resolve puts *that* out of the question . . .' Being comfortable mentally mattered more for the moment than being comfortable financially; so it looked as though the project would have to be shelved.

But here as everywhere, Charlotte's death changed everything. Well might Madame de St Laurent collapse and faint that morning; for now besides the ever-present problem of debt the Duke could and would justify separation to himself on the grounds that his country called him, that it was his duty to England. Through some peculiar personal logic the Duke had always reconciled his ridiculous self-indulgence with a belief in himself as an unrecognised, unrewarded model of self-sacrifice to the nation. He was wont to speak of 'my life of gloom and struggle'. Now in his country's dire hour of need, with the security of the succession threatened, he was prepared to make the supreme sacrifice of marrying into solvency. This led him to summon Thomas Creevey, MP for Thetford, to Brussels in December 1817, to communicate his wishes to the government. His choice of a confidant shows how little Kent grasped the realities of contemporary British politics; Creevey, a brilliantly irreverent diarist and intimate friend of the Royal Family's great critic the Duke of Wellington, could hardly contain his laughter as the Duke spoke, and immediately afterwards recorded Kent's preposterous proposals in order to share the joke with his friends:

'. . . The Duke began, to my great surprise, a conversation with me upon the derangement of the succession of the throne by this event, and of the necessity of the unmarried Princes becoming married, if the crown was to be kept in their family; and having in addition asked him, I believe, what he thought the Regent would do on the subject of a divorce, and whether he thought the Duke of Clarence would marry, the D of K to the best of my recollection, and I would almost say word for word, spoke to me as follows:-

'"My opinion is the Regent will not attempt a divorce. I know persons in the Cabinet who will never consent to such

[71]

a measure. Then, was he to attempt it, his conduct would be exposed to such recriminations as to make him unpopular, beyond all measure, throughout the country. No: he will never attempt it. Besides, the crime of adultery on her part must be proved in an English court of justice, and if found guilty she must be executed for high treason. No: the Regent will never try for a divorce.

'"As for the Duke of York, at his time of life and that of the Duchess, all issue, of course, is out of question. The Duke of Clarence, I have no doubt, will marry if he can; but the terms he asks from the Ministers are such as they can never comply with. Besides a settlement such as is proper for a Prince who marries expressly for a succession to the Throne, the Duke of Clarence demands the payment of all his debts, which are very great, and a handsome provisions for each of his ten natural children. These are terms that no Ministers can accede to. Should the Duke of Clarence not marry, the next Prince in succession is myself; and altho' I trust I shall be at all times ready to obey any call my country may make upon me, God only knows the sacrifice it will be to make, whenever I shall think it my duty to become a married man. It is now seven-and-twenty years that Madame St Laurent and I have lived together; we are of the same age, and have been in all climates, and in all difficulties together; and you may well imagine, Mr Creevey, the pang it will occasion me to part with her. I put it to your own feeling – the event of any separation between you and Mrs Creevey . . . As for Mme St L herself I protest I don't know what is to become of her if a marriage is to be forced upon me; her feelings are already so agitated upon the subject. You saw, no doubt, that unfortunate paragraph in the *Morning Chronicle*, which appeared within a day or two after the Pss. Charlotte's death; and in which my marrying was alluded to. Upon receiving the paper containing that article at the same time with my private letters, I did as is my constant practice, I threw the newspaper across the table to Mme St L, and began to open and read my letters. I had not done so but a very short time when my attention was called to an extraordinary noise

[72]

and a strong convulsive movement in Mme St L's throat. For a short time I entertained serious apprehensions for her safety; and when, upon her recovery, I enquired into the occasion of this attack, she pointed to the article in the *Morning Chronicle* relating to my marriage.

'"From that day to this I am compelled to be in the practice of daily dissimulation with Mme St L, to keep this subject from her thoughts. I am fortunately acquainted with the gentlemen in Bruxelles who conduct the Liberal and Oracle newspapers; they have promised me to keep all articles upon the subject of my marriage out of their papers, and I hope my friends in England will be equally prudent. My brother the Duke of Clarence is the elder brother, and has certainly the right to marry if he chooses, and I would not interfere with him on any account. If he wishes to be King – to be married and have children, poor man – God help him! let him do so. For myself – I am a man of no ambition, and wish only to remain as I am . . . Easter, you know, falls v. early this year – 22 March. If the D. of Clarence does not take any step before that time, I must find some pretext to reconcile Mme St L to my going to England for a short time. St George's Day is the day now fixed for keeping the birthday, and my paying my respects to the Regent on that day will be a sufficient excuse for my appearing in England. When once there, it will be easy for me to consult with my friends as to the proper steps to be taken. Should the D. of Clarence do nothing before that time as to marrying, it will become my duty no doubt, to take some measures upon the subject myself."

'"You have heard the names of the Pss. of Baden and the Prss. of Saxe-Coburg mentioned."

'"The latter connection would perhaps be the better of the two, fr. the circumstance of Prince Leopold being so popular with the nation; but before anything is proceeded with in this matter, I shall hope & Expect to see justice done by Nation & the Ministers to Mme St L. She is of v. good family & has never been an actress, & I am the first and only person who ever lived with her. Her disinterestedness, too, has been equal to her fidelity. When she first came to me it was upon £100 a year. That sum was afterwards raised to £400, & finally to £1000; but when my debts made it necessary for me to sacrifice a great part of my income, Mme St L insisted upon again returning to her income of £400 a year. If Mme St L is to return to live amongst her friends, it must be in such a state of independence as to command their respect. I shall not require v. much, but a certain no. of servants & a carriage are essentials. Whatever the Ministers agree to give for such purposes must be put out of all doubt as to its continuance. I shall name Mr Brougham, yourself and two other people on behalf of Mme St L for this object.

'"As to my own settlement, as I shall marry (if I marry at all) for the succession, I shall expect the Duke of York's marriage to be considered the precedent. That was a marriage for the succession & £25,000 for income was settled, in addition to all his other income, purely on that account. I shall be contented with the same arrangement, without making any demands grounded upon the difference of the value of money in 1792 & at present. As for the payment of my debts, I don't call them great. The nation, on the contrary, is greatly my debtor."'

But by the end of November, as John Croker, another MP and diarist, told Robert Peel:

'. . . A propos of royal matches, I hear that Ministers have been a little puzzled how to deal with the avowed readiness of the Duke of Kent to sacrifice himself and jump into the matrimonial gulf for the good of his country, but they have hit upon a scheme which seems politic. They propose to marry the Duke of Clarence, as the eldest unmarried Prince, and he who has a right to the first chance; and also to marry the Duke of Cambridge, the youngest unmarried Prince, from whom the country has the best chance; and having thus resolved to burn the candle at both ends, Vansittart (the Chancellor of the Exchequer) discovers that he cannot afford to burn it in the middle too, and therefore Kent and Sussex cannot have the wedding establishments etc. suited to their rank.'

The Chancellor was against providing expensive households for the Dukes as he had to abolish the property tax which was only levied during time of war.

*   *   *

VII
No Time Will be Lost

Winter 1817–18

Elsewhere, the winter of 1817 had seen Kent's brothers manfully throwing themselves into the gap caused by Charlotte's death.

As Peter Pindar wrote:

> *'Agog are we all, both old and young*
> *Warm'd with desire to be prolific*
> *And prompt with resolution strong*
> *To fight in Hymen's war terrific.'*

Even before the funeral had taken place, the Princes began the hunt for suitable brides. First off the mark was the youngest of all the Dukes, the forty-three-year-old Duke of Cambridge, known to his sisters as 'Dolly', 'Dear Dolly Dowsy'. Good-looking, with a blond wig, he was diligent and honest; he rose at six, he read the lesson at church, never went to fat like his brothers, and paid his bills on time. He was so affable, pleasant and modest that history has recorded little criticism of him, though the Princess of Wales was snide about his commonplace appearance: 'He looks like a sergeant, and so vulgar with his ears full of powder.'

Hanover had nearly always been his home. After years of careful study at Göttingen University, he served in the Hanoverian Army and unsuccessfully defended the state against Napoleon. The inhabitants welcomed the conqueror. The Duke fled to England where he waited till 1813 to return as Governor-General of Hanover and enjoyed his life as a bachelor.

'He keeps us all alive with his good humour and affability,' wrote a contemporary in Hanover. 'He runs about just like a private gentleman and will dine with you or drink with you as may be most convenient. His rage for music is quite extraordinary . . . he cannot speak of his father without tears in his eyes . . .'

Now the most pleasant of all the brothers felt it his duty to preserve the dynasty, and without delay chose the beautiful Princess Augusta of Hesse-Cassel as a suitable bride. She was the youngest daughter of the Landgrave of Hesse-Cassel and the great-grand-daughter of George II of England. (Her sister was married to the Duke of Mecklenburg-Strelitz, whose sister in turn was the notorious bride of the Duke of Cumberland, so the match would set up an elaborate symmetry.) Within two weeks of Charlotte's death Cambridge wrote to the Prince Regent thanking him for sending a letter permitting proposals to be made. The Regent's consent was necessary under the Royal Marriages Act.

Speedy horses took the request from Hanover to Hesse-Cassel and ten days later the newly betrothed Duke of Cambridge was once again writing to his brother:

'. . . Though I feel that this is a moment I ought not to worry you with my concerns, yet after all your kindness to me I can not let the mail leave Hanover without informing you that I have sent my proposals to the Princess Augusta, and have received a favourable answer the day before yesterday. I of course do not think of going to Cassel till the deep mourning is over, and indeed I should have preferred waiting till I could have spoke to the Princess myself, but as there has been several months ago a report spread about my marriage which will undoubtedly (be) renewed, so I thought it more delicate the moment I received your sanction to write at once to the Landgrave Fredrick and his daughter stating at the same time my earnest wish that the whole should be kept a profound secret till I could go myself to Cassel. I trust, my dearest brother, that you will approve of what I have done: my intention at least was to act with delicacy by all parties, and I trust that you will see it in that light . . . though far from you, my dearest brother, I have not felt the less for you, for neither time nor distance can ever alter the affection . . .'

Cambridge was waiting for 'black glove mourning' to pass so that he could with propriety publicly visit the Princess to formally ask her hand in marriage 'merely for etiquette and custom's sake'. Meanwhile the Prince Regent was plotting the courses of his other brothers' marriages.

A complex and voluminous correspondence opened between the Regent, his mother who was again taking the waters at Bath, the Duke of Cambridge and the Duke of Clarence, discussing how to marry off the latter. Everyone agreed it was desirable; Clarence wanted it himself, but first he had to make *absolutely clear* what his *position* was:–

> 'If the *Cabinet* consider the measure of *my* marrying one of consequence they *ought* to state to *me* what they *can* and *will* propose for my establishment: for *without previously* being acquainted with *their* intentions as to *money* matters *I cannot* and *will* not make any positive offer to any Princess. I have *ten* children *totally* and *entirely* dependent on myself: I owe *forty thousand* pounds of *funded* debt for which of course I pay interest, and I have a *floating* debt of *sixteen thousand* pounds: in addition to *all which* if I *marry* I must have a town house and my house at Bushey compleately repaired and *entirely* new furnished . . . If *that* settlement is made which I can consider *adequate* I shall *only* have to explain my *real* situation as the *fond* and *attached* father of *ten* children to the Princess whom I am to marry: for without a *complete* understanding of my *full* determination to see *when* and *where* I please *my daughters* I *cannot and will not* marry.'

As long as *that* was *understood*, Cambridge could proceed with his diplomatic efforts to obtain the hand of his new bride's sister, Amelia of Hesse-Cassel, for his petulant and demanding brother. But his efforts were unrewarded; after months of delicate negotiations, the Electoral Prince, her father, replied: 'I must observe to your Royal Highness that both the youth of my daughter and her delicate constitution, together with the advanced years and numerous family of the Duke of Clarence, make me hope that no proposal of marriage in this direction will be forthcoming.' Clarence had a long history of matrimonial rejections. After twenty years of living with Mrs Jordan, the mother of his ten children, he discarded her because he needed an increased allowance and he also realised that the Electorate of Hanover (which under Salic law descended only through the male line) would almost certainly fall to him, so he wanted a legitimate heir. Free of Mrs Jordan, he pursued Miss Catherine Tilney-Long of Ramsgate, 'a lovely nice little angel' all the lovelier for her £40,000 a year. She was not dazzled by the ardour or rank of this ageing boorish debtor and, one after another, turned down six proposals.

Not to be daunted, Clarence proffered his hand to Miss Margaret Elphinstone, and met a refusal 'in the most decided and peremptory terms'. The Duke of Gloucester's sister, Sophia, disdained him, and the Dowager Lady Downshire was dismissive. He had no better luck with Lady Lindsay, and Lady Berkeley found him 'impossible'.

Negotiations were conducted with a view to allying the undisposable Duke to the sister of the Tsar of Russia. The delays and delicacy of these were very trying to his oafish nature. As the Russian Ambassador's wife, Princess Lieven, was leaving a ball, he charged after her, knocked her footman aside and jumped into her elegant carriage. 'Are you hot, Madame?' 'No, Monseigneur.' 'Are you cold, Madame?' 'No, Monseigneur.' 'May I hold your hand?' The Princess, a lady of some beauty and wit, knew the Royal reputation for insanity, and feared she was about to be raped. But the Duke's wildness turned out to be solely connected with the outcome of the marriage negotiations: he just wanted to know what she thought. She thought he was an imbecile, and wrote as much in her letters back to St Petersburg: the proposal accordingly came to nothing.

Now, in 1818, the government turned to Denmark as a possible solution – Denmark had provided a wife for James I and a dull husband for Queen Anne. On 7 February it was reported that 'a matrimonial regotiation is on the *tapis* between His Royal Highness the Duke of Clarence and Princess Anne of Denmark'. On the 20th the *Morning Chronicle* announced: 'We can now state with confidence that the object of the line of battleships bound for Copenhagen, which we have previously alluded to, is to bring to

England Her Serene Highness the Princess of Denmark, the affianced bride of the Duke of Clarence.' But no: the battleships must turn back; for on the 24th 'the union is broken off by the refusal of Her Serene Highness'.

Perhaps she had heard rumours from Brighton: here the old man was pursuing a matrimonial policy of his own. On 9 February he had been reported as present at the 'ball and supper for one hundred persons, given at No. 1 the Old Steine by the worthy Miss *Wykeham*'. Miss Wykeham was an heiress with £16,000 a year from Thame Park, Oxfordshire. Clarence had set eyes on her on a recent visit to Brighton and fallen violently in love. This was a habit of his from early in life. On several occasions in his youth, the King, his father, had been forced to pack him off in a boat when he had impetuously offered his hand to young ladies of common stock.

Now, at fifty-two, he set his heart on Sophia Wykeham, a lady of some character who was later described as half-mad and was at this time 'a delighter in field sports, and an excellent horsewoman, for which she has recently got the name of High Wickham'. He declared to her that he was without a penny in the world but – if it would please her to be Duchess of Clarence and maybe one day Queen of England, he would be happy to convey the honours. It did please her. Could it be that at long last he had found a wife?

It was not simple. The news of the match was received as a disaster at court, as Clarence's sister Princess Mary wrote in a letter to the Prince Regent:

> 'The Queen is half *distracted* just having received William's letter in which he tells her he has proposed and been accepted by Miss Wickham and will be at Windsor tomorrow . . . she *desires not* to *see him* untill she has seen you . . . William said he was determined to go through with it and that he was certain the Act of Parliament was such that he should carry the point & all England with him . . . I told him I was sure it would break the Queen's heart . . .'

'Clarence has been near dying,' was the news from Lord

Folkestone writing to Creevey on 23 February 1818. He was all passion and desperation; four days earlier he had turned up suddenly at Miss Wykeham's villa in Marine Parade, where he dined and spent the evening and 'walked her about till her pellisse hung loose on her'. 'This unexpected arrival, followed by the departure of the Duke, as well as the amiable and opulent heiress, for London, has given rise to much speculation,' said the press. On the 25th the marriage with Miss Wykeham was announced to be finally arranged.

Fremantle was writing to Buckingham:

'There is a grand emotion in the Royal Family, and with some reason. The Duke of Clarence has thought proper to propose to Miss Wykeham who has accepted him. The Prince, accompanied by his sister the Duchess of Gloucester, went to Windsor on Tuesday to inform the Queen of this *happy event*, who was of course outrageous. The Council have sat twice upon the business; and it is determined, as I understand, to oppose it. I don't know whether you know Miss W————; she is a fine vulgar Miss.'

The Regent and Government were not going to admit vulgarity into the Royal Family without a fight.

*   *   *

VIII

Love's Labours Lost

February 1818

The repercussions of Charlotte's death were coming in on all all sides. While Clarence bustled between Brighton and London, and Kent hustled a profitable escape from Mme de St Laurent, scandal broke from an entirely unexpected direction.

On 12 February Sir Richard Croft spent the night in a house in Wimpole Street in order to attend the confinement of the wife of the clergyman, Dr Thackeray. The house belonged to Mrs Thackeray's sister. As the labour lingered on hour after hour, he became quite beside himself and exclaimed: 'If you are anxious, what must I be?'

On the Friday morning, 13 February, the child had not been born and Sir Richard went upstairs to rest. When he did not come downstairs a servant went upstairs and found him on a bed, flat on his back, with a pistol in each hand; the muzzles of both were at either side of his head. A shocking spectacle presented itself: 'The body of Sir Richard Croft was lying on the bed, shockingly mangled; his arms extended over his breast, and a pistol in each hand. One of the pistols had been loaded with slugs, the other with ball. Both were discharged, and the head of the unfortunate gentleman was literally blown to pieces,' wrote a correspondent in the *Morning Chronicle*. He had fired two shots simultaneously and blown out his brains. On a table beside the bed lay Shakespeare's play, *Love's Labours Lost*, which was open at a page in which appeared the words: 'Good God! Where is the Princess?'

Mrs Thackeray's child was safely delivered. Sir Richard's body was taken away for an autopsy. A coroner's inquest was held and

[83]

depositions taken revealed that ever since the Princess Charlotte's death croft had been in a state of the deepest anxiety and excitement bordering on insanity. But it was stressed that although the fifty-six-year-old doctor had been suffering from great depression of spirits he had never in his former life shown any symptoms of insanity.

It was now a triple obstetric tragedy – mother, baby and accoucheur, all dead, all victims of bad midwifery practice. Charlotte's death and the rumours that were afloat were too much for Croft – rather like the captain of the ship that had sunk, he felt he had to go down with it. 'The circumstances produced no ordinary sensation,' wrote the *Morning Chronicle*. 'Suspicions were aroused by a concerted attempt to suppress all knowledge of the manner of Sir Richard's death.' Reporters were refused access to the inquest.

Not only did Croft's death bring back all the stories of Princess Charlotte which had begun to subside, but the gossip about the birth of the Duke of Devonshire was revived. Croft had gone to Paris to attend the late Duchess of Devonshire. It was said that a girl was born but it was swapped with a boy. The story of the Devonshire baby-swapping was circulated to such a degree that it was even mentioned – and dismissed – in Croft's obituary.

Mr W. Fremantle was again reporting to his friend the Marquis of Buckingham:

'. . . Croft's death was a sudden frenzy. It is quite unaccountable, how much the story about the Duke of Devonshire is believed – really, not a house in London, but where I hear it; you know, I suppose, what it is. The present Duchess, who is become devoté, is said to have confessed the changing the child at the time of the late Duchess's accouchement, and that the present Duke is not the child born; who is, I can't learn – but either Mrs Lamb or Captain Clifford. So much for this story, which you may credit or not. I don't one word, but thousands do . . . Croft destroying himself now, of course, adds to the story and belief . . . .'

Alas Croft was buried – but not the rumours. He was laid down in the Croft family vaults in St James's, Piccadilly.

The unfortunate man who had paid such a price for getting his name in the history books was to all appearances an unlikely candidate for suicide. He was descended from the ancient and distinguished family who owned Croft Castle in Herefordshire, with a title of Baronet since 1671. He had 'discovered marks of a comprehensive intelligence' as an apprentice doctor, had been a pupil at St Bartholomew's and a surgeon in Oxford. He had married the daughter of Dr Denman, one of the most fashionable accoucheurs in London, and gradually taken over his father-in-law's practice. He was able to leave his wife and four children a handsome amount in his will. It was an unexceptional private success story that had been caught up in an extraordinary national maelstrom, and dragged to death in its wake.

The vital witness to Charlotte's death was now out of the way. Had it been Croft's fault or was there a curse on the reigning Queens of England and aspirant Queens? Although there have been six Queen regnants in English history – Mary, Elizabeth, Anne, Mary, Victoria and the present Queen – Victoria is the only reigning Queen of England to be succeeded by her own issue.

★   ★   ★

IX
Enter Humbug
Winter/Spring 1818

S uddenly, Princess Elizabeth was to be married. All heads
turned amazed in a new direction. Princess Elizabeth was forty-
seven and the dearest of her mother's children. She had always
been at the Queen's side and was the one bright star of 'the
sisterhood', the only one who could keep the cantankerous old lady
from sinking into gloom. Now she announced that she was to go
off with the Prince of Hesse-Homburg, and it seemed certain that
this drastic removal – whether it was for the succession, for
affection, or out of sheer desperation – would break her mother's
heart.

Elizabeth had grown dreadfully fat during her long years of
spinsterhood, but she had a vivacity, charm and wit that endeared
her to all who knew her. For the past eight years she had leased a
'cottage with a meadow for a cow' at Old Windsor from a local
grocer. Here, in this tiny cottage with such low ceilings that a
man in the parlour 'stood almost as high as the ceiling', she often
entertained her family at 'hay homes' and tended her pigs and
sheep. Once referring to some pigs sent from the Queen to her
Lady-in-Waiting, Lady Holdernesse, she wrote:

'. . . My dear Lady Mary . . . Mamma has ordered two pigs
which have been born and bred at Frogmore to be sent up by
tomorrow morning's early stage for her. She flatters herself
that dreary Lady H will like them; you may laugh . . . but I am
not a little proud of receiving the commission from Mamma
as the Farmyard is my Hobby Horse. Pray tell Lady Mary that

the Pigs are of the Chinese breed which makes them look so small . . .'

She was very talented and a series of engravings from her own designs were published: *Cupid Turned Volunteer* accompanied by *Poetical Illustrations* by Thomas Park, FSA, and in 1806 *The Birth and Triumph of Love* and another series *The Power and Progress of Genius* dedicated to Queen Charlotte.

Elizabeth was also a wit as illustrated by this letter to Lady Harcourt:

'. . . Anything so disgusting as the breakfast at Woodsgate' Inn, on the way fr Weymouth, I thank God I never saw before and never wish to see again – bad butter, Tea, Coffee, bread &c: nothing to touch but boil'd eggs, which were so hard that I cld not eat them. So I returned to the carriage just as I got out – starved. However, having wisely followed Sir Francis Wronghead's ways, and had a large Plumb Cake put up as Stowage for the Stomach, I rejoiced much at the thought of seizing this when I got back to the Coach; but the moment I had prepared myself in Battle array, with a knife in my hand to begin the massacre, they told me it was for Mamma, and my knife returned innocent to my Pocket.

'As I was not allowed to eat, I determined like a true woman to talk. Lord Harcourt and you served as our constant to unpick; and we all agreed how sorry we were to have quitted you. When the conversation runs on the subject of those one truly loves, all unpleasant rememberances are at an end; so I forgot my hunger, and you served as a Breakfast. I was then, you perceive, satisfied, and got through Salisbury, Andover, and Overton vastly well, and very much contented to get to Hartford Bridge, where our dinner quite made up for our breakfast; for I never ate a better anywhere. The bottle went round as on board our dear Juno; and the first toast was to all our friends we had quitted, and then to the Juno . . .

'Mama has ordered my younger Sisters to stay at home today – they cough so – but otherwise everybody is well. We began going to Chaple this morning; it must be wholesome, it is so disagreeable. However, this is a life of trials, God knows it is; so I hope to be rewarded in the next . . .

Yours affectionate,

Eliza

'I enclose you a new Vocabulary, which has just come out:–

Vernacular Terms	*Fashionable Sense*
Age	An infirmity nobody knows
Conscience	Something to swear by
Country	A place for Pigs and Poultry
Day	Night
Night	Day
Debt	A necessary evil
Dining	Keeping up appearances
Dinner	Supper
Dressed	Half-naked
London	The most delightful place!
Lounging	Daily occupation
Modest	Sheepish
New	Delightful
Pay	Only applied to visits
Prayers	The cant of silly people
Christianity	Having a pew at Church
Time	Only applied to Music
Protection	Keeping a Mistress
Vice	Only applied to Horses
Undress	Complete clothing
Gossip	Amusing conversation
Work	A vulgarism'

The man for whom this lively, perceptive woman was to uproot herself, Frederick of Hesse-Homburg, had no other admirers in England. He was a public laughing-stock. No one could understand her choice except as another desperate old maid's flight from the clutches of the Queen. Accounts of him on his introduction to English society were unflattering:– 'a gross corpulent German of enormous dimensions, smelling always of tobacco' . . . 'forty-nine and as fat as herself' . . . 'an unpleasing husband (in looks at least)' . . . 'he snores at the theatres' . . . 'you never saw such a disgusting object' . . . 'I have just seen H H at the Levee; and an uglier hound with a snout buried in hair, I ne'er saw' . . . 'it is impossible to describe the monster of a man – a vulgar-looking German corporal, whose breath and hide is a compound between tobacco and garlic. What can have induced her nobody can guess; he has about £300 per annum. It will be a dreadful blow to her (the Queen) and I should not wonder if after the Princess is gone she sinks under it. She is much altered, and, I think, breaking fast.'

Frederick had written in 1804 to ask for the hand of one of George III's daughters, but for some reason (that is not recorded) the offer wasn't pursued – or was dropped.

It was not without surprise that the Prince Regent heard on 28 January that the Prince of Hesse-Homburg had arrived in London 'for the purpose of soliciting the hand of the Princess Elizabeth'. Immediately Elizabeth received a letter of proposal which horrified the Queen. The Princess wrote to her brother:

'. . . I therefore candidly own I wish to accept this offer. I am no longer young, and fairly feel that having my own home will be a comfort in time, tho' it causes me a degree of pain, which I feel *deeply* – more than I have words to express – but God knows our lives have been lives of *trial* and ever will be so. I have tried to the utmost of my power to do my Duty as a daughter and sister. I pray the Almighty to strengthen me in those of a *wife* . . .'

On 29 January, Elizabeth told her mother, and at first the Queen's response was heartening: 'You always wished to settle,' she said, 'and have always said that you thought a woman might be happier and more comfortable in having a home.' But her illness and depression rendered her inconsistent and her attitude to Elizabeth during the next ten days rendered the unfortunate woman prostrate. 'Believe me,' wrote Elizabeth to the Regent, 'my mother is so angry that it frightens me . . . says she is so incensed by my conduct that she cannot bear to see me.' The Regent visited Windsor to calm his mother, but only temporarily – two days after his departure Elizabeth wrote to him saying that she had difficulty doing so as her eyes were 'completely blinded for tears'. Another visit – more diplomacy and attention – and the Queen was sufficiently soothed to enable her to speak to Elizabeth again, after first having sent her a diamond necklace by way of apology. Upset and distressed by her mother's behaviour she might be, but Elizabeth was still acute enough to note that her mother '. . . has been very comfortable with others when I am away, before me she tries to be worse'.

So the engagement was finally announced in the Court Circular – but not before Elizabeth had had to agree to stay in the country for some time after her marriage, so that her mother would not be deprived of her company.

There remained the problem of presenting 'Humbug' to London society. He made a grotesque entry; a correspondent describes a particularly unfortunate visit:–

'The Queen had yesterday a drawing-room to exhibit the Prince of Hesse . . . I heard that a few evenings ago, the Queen dropt her fan at York House, and Humbug stooped with so much alacrity to pick it up that the exertion created so parlous a slit and produced such a display that nothing was left to the bride's imagination . . . nothing remained but for the Royal brothers to interpose their screen, and for him to retire as fast as he could. It was then proposed that he should go home, but he declined this, "as the Duke of York was so much more large, dat he vas sure his breeches would go on over all". The valet was called, the Duke's breeches drawn on over the poor remains of Humbug's and succeeded to admiration.'

But despite the disasters and ridicule the Princess's perseverance in matrimony was not to be shaken, and she declared 'it was the goal she had always looked forward to' and was said to be 'really in love, and blushed rosy red when the Prince Hesse entered the room'.

She was really too young for her second childhood, but her

[91]

trousseau was that more usual for a nubile girl: Pomona green, lilac and white striped satin, white kerseymere and fine Indian muslin. For the wedding, on 7 April, the substantial Princess wore a court dress in rich silver tissue with flounces of Brussels lace, and sported a head-dress of ostrich feathers. The bridegroom was in his general's uniform. The ceremony began at 7 p.m. in the Throne Room at Buckingham House. In front of the throne was a temporary altar covered in crimson velvet and arrayed with a profusion of golden plate. Gout caused the absence of the Regent; lunacy that of the King. The Duke of York gave the bride away.

Even in 1818, Royal weddings appealed to rebels and republicans. Here is the obsequious account of the American Minister, Mr Rush:

'April 8. 1818. The Princess Elizabeth was married last evening to the Prince of Hesse Homberg. The cabinet ministers foreign ambassadors and ministers, officers of the Royal household, persons in the suites of the Royal Dukes and Princesses, the Archbishops of Canterbury and York, the Bishop of London, the Lord Chancellor, the Lord Chief Justice were present. The Prince Regent was not there, being ill. Our invitation was from the Queen, given through the Earl of Winchelsea, nearly three weeks before. We got to the palace at seven o'clock. Pages were on the stairs to conduct us to the rooms. The ceremony took place in the throne-room. There was a salver of great size on which was represented the Lord's Supper. The company being assembled, the bridegroom entered, with his attendants. Then came the Queen, with the bride and royal family. All approached the altar. Her majesty sat; the rest stood. The marriage service was read by the Archbishop of Canterbury. The Duke of York gave the bride away. The whole was according to the forms of the church, and performed with great solemnity. A record of the marriage was made. When all was finished, the bride knelt before the Queen to receive her blessing.

'Soon after the service was performed the bride and bridegroom set off for Windsor. The company remained. The evening passed in high ceremony, without excluding social ease. From the members of the royal family the guests had every measure of courtesy. The conduct of the Queen was remarkable. This venerable personage, the head of a large family – her children then clustering about her – the female head of a great empire, in the 76th year of her age, went the rounds of the company, speaking to all. There was a kindliness in her manner from which time had struck away useless forms. No one did she omit. Around her neck hung a miniature portrait of the King. He was absent, scathed by the hand of Heaven; a marriage going on in one of his palaces; he, the lonely, suffering tenant of another. But the portrait was a token superior to a crown! It bespoke the natural glory of wife and mother, eclipsing the artificial glory of queen. For more than fifty years this royal pair had lived together in affection. The scene would have been one of interest anywhere. May it not be noticed on a throne?

'Tea was handed. The Queen continued to stand, or move about the rooms. In one was a table of refreshments. I went to it with Major-General Sir Henry Torrens, distinguished by service and wounds, whose acquaintance I had made at Lord Bathurst's. He was of the establishment of the Duke of York. On the table were urns and tea-kettles of fretted gold. Sir Henry recommended me to a glass of what I supposed wine, in a flagon near me; but he called it king's cup, given only at royal weddings.

'Returning to the chief rooms, the Princess Sophia Matilda pointed out to Mrs. Rush and myself the paintings, the representation of a bird from India formed of precious stones so as to resemble beautiful plumage, with other objects of curiosity or taste. She did more. She spoke of Washington. She paid a spontaneous tribute to his virtues. None but Americans can know how this would fall upon the heart. To hear his immortal name pronounced with praise in a palace of George III, had a high and touching value. Mentioning this Princess, I add, that myself and family afterwards experienced her obliging attentions in ways the remembrance of which is cherished with grateful pleasure. At ten the company came away.'

As soon as the ceremony was concluded, forty-one rounds of cannon fire were shot from St James's Palace to celebrate the joyous event. And in answer forty-one rounds were discharged from the cannon at the Tower of London.

More graphic than Rush's unctuous notes is the alternative account given by Mrs Mangles, the widow of George III's chaplain:

'The Duke of York led the Queen, the Prince Regent not being quite recovered from his gout . . . Then came the Hero, the Prince Hesse Homburg, he went up to the communion table and stood 10 minutes alone . . . then walked in the Bride . . . the Duke of York gave her away and behaved very *bad*. The Prince Homburg thought when he said "I will" very loud and distinct, all was done, but the Archbishop desired him to repeat after him . . . He cannot speak English and made such works of it, it was then the Duke of York laughed so, he was obliged to stuff his handkerchief in his mouth to conceal it. He promised to "lof her" . . . the hero was most unheroically sick when driving away . . .'

Humbug was certainly the comic star of the show. Everyone had stories of him. Before the wedding, one correspondent wrote, 'they immersed him several times in a warm bath to make him a little clean; and they kept him three days from smoking, which, as he smoked five pipes a day, was great forbearance. But as he was married yesterday, he has probably resumed that indulgence now.'

For the journey to Windsor in a 'landaulet and four' Homburg changed into full ball dress and the fat bride put on a white satin pelisse with a veil.

'. . . She is delighted with her hero as she calls him. On his way from the marriage ceremony to the Regent's Cottage, where, to his great annoyance, they were destined to pass the first quarter of the honeymoon, he was sick, from being unused to a close carriage, and forced to leave her for the dickey, and put

Baron O'Nagten in his place. He said he was not so much ennuyé at the Cottage as he expected, having passed all his time in his dressing gown and slippers, smoking in the conservatory.'

The honeymoon lingered on at Windsor with the bridegroom smoking in the Gothic conservatory. The departure to Germany was postponed so as not to give alarm to the Queen, whose health was failing. It was generally believed – not least by her – that the shock of her favourite daughter leaving her forever would send her to her grave.

The Prince of Hesse-Homburg was enjoying his new-found importance. The 316 square kilometres of Hesse-Homburg had only 22,000 inhabitants under a monarchical Government. The Prince's father, the Landgrave, was desperately poor, and the castle was in a sadly dilapidated state. Princess Elizabeth's jointure of £6000 a year from England would be most welcome.

★   ★   ★

Elsewhere in Germany, the first contestant to get going in the Royal reproduction race should by now have passed the marriage post. But the Duke of Cambridge's wedding was delayed because he was waiting for news from England about the increase in his allowance. Since February the poor Duke had been very embarrassed financially by having to rent lodgings and hire horses in Cassel while waiting for word from England. If he married before his finances were debated it would jeopardise his chance of an increased allowance. The Regent was neglecting to put the question of Cambridge's grant before Parliament.

As early as 31 December the Duke had written to the Regent about the date of the marriage which, 'I am aware, must depend upon the message you send to Parliament; and I shall depend upon you . . . for letting me know when I am at liberty to fix the day.'

Three months later, on 2 March, poor Cambridge was very impatient indeed waiting for news from England. He wrote accusingly to his brother pointing out that the agony over the delay 'becomes more painful every day from the total ignorance I have been kept in when my marriage is to take place'. He reminded the Prince that approval for the marriage proposals had been so prompt that 'I certainly did believe that the message would have been sent to Parliament early enough for me to have received your consent under the Great Seal by the middle of this month, so that at the end of it the wedding might have taken place, and we would have been in England in April, time enough to be at the Drawing-Room on the 23rd.'

In his cautious, self-righteous tones he complained to his brother that the delay had caused him great additional expense and that he resented being held back by the unmarriageable Clarence:

'Far be it from me to wish to prevent William or any of my brothers from marrying, but really it is too hard to make my marriage dependent on theirs, especially when it appears that there is a great difficulty in finding a bride for them. God knows what will be the answer from Meiningen; should it be un-favourable, I must entreat you again, my dearest brother, not to keep my marriage any longer back.'

He went on to point out that the bride's family, the Hesse-Cassels, were 'astonished at the ignorance I have been kept in on a point so highly interesting to them'.

But the debate on marriage allowances was not held until mid-April, when Cambridge could be considered together with his two elder brothers. Consequently the marriage had to wait till 7 May, a month after Elizabeth's.

When at last it came, it was the happiest of days for the Duke, whose dynastic arrangement had turned into a love-match; 'every hour of my life do I feel my attachment and affection increase for my bride' he had told his brother. After the ceremony, he set off with his new wife and his father-in-law, 'a venerable old gentleman of seventy', on the road to England.

*   *   *

Princess Elizabeth, late
Landgravine of Hesse-Homburg,
by Sir William Beechey, 1797

Princess Augusta by Peter Edward
Stroehling, 1807

Children of George III, detail from portrait of Queen Charlotte by
Benjamin West

Queen Charlotte by Edward Stroehling, 1807

The Prince of Wales, later the Prince Regent, later George IV, by
Sir Thomas Lawrence

Edward Augustus, Duke of Kent,
by George Dawe, 1818

Duke of Clarence, later William
IV, by Sir Martin Archer-Shee,
1833

Duke of Cambridge by Thomas
Lawrence

Augustus, Duke of Sussex, by
B. S. Marks.

Princess Charlotte and Prince Leopold by George Dawe

The COURT at Brighton à la Chinese !!

Exercising a Hobby from Wales to Hertford !!

THE MATRIMONIAL MANIA — or — Poor Jonny Ridden to Death.

PRINCELY AMUSEMENTS OR THE HUMORS OF THE FAMILY.

Sir Richard Croft in his coffin,
by Sir Thomas Lawrence

A SCENE in the New FARCE called the RIVALS or a Visit to the Heir Presumptive.

BRIGHTON HOT BATH, or Preparations for The WEDDING!!

Miss MARY & her loving Cousin! or SINGLE GLOUCESTER prefer'd to German Sausage!!

Princess Caroline, 'the damned Princess of Wales', depicted by a contemporary cartoonist with her lover, Bergami

The Genius of History, or dressing for a Masked Ball at Naples.

Buckingham House by Antony
Vandyke Copley Fielding

Claremont

Kensington Palace

The winner: The Duchess of Kent and
Princess Alexandrina Victoria, later Queen Victoria

X

Prize Money

Like Cambridge, Elizabeth had managed to find love within the terms of the Royal Marriages Act, seeing charms in her Humbug that were hidden to everyone else. Brother and sister had each in their ways made happy marriages. William, the Duke of Clarence, was not so lucky. He would have moved heaven and earth for Sophia Wykeham; but moving the British government was another matter. At the beginning of March he had dropped the appeal he meant to make before Parliament for his marriage to her. He was going to announce it officially to the Privy Council, and sent notification, but before it was entered the Regent and the Chancellor urged him strongly to reconsider it. He prevaricated and asked for a long day to consider. But his mother and his brothers kept up such an attack that at last, fuming but ineffectual, he gave up the whole matter.

He had held out with good reason: Miss Wykeham had been the first woman out of eighteen to say yes to his matrimonial proposals. But his family had arranged a consolation prize. On 21 March a resigned old man imparted the news to his oldest bastard son:

'I have delayed till the last moment writing in hopes of being able to inform you who is to be the Duchess of Clarence. I can now with *truth* tho' not with *satisfaction* my heart being with Miss Wykeham. It is to be the Princess of Saxe-Meiningen, whose *beauty* and *character* are *universally* acknowledged. She is doomed *poor, dear innocent young* creature to be my wife. I *cannot, I will not, I must not* ill use her . . . What time may produce in my heart I cannot tell, but at present I *think* and exist only for Miss Wykeham. But enough of your father's misery.'

D

The press could hardly believe that the harum-scarum search for a partner was over. On 7 April, they were putting it out that yet another Princess had turned him down: 'Rumours say that the Princess of Hesse-Cassel has declined the proffered hand of the Duke of Clarence, and that a union is on the *tapis* between His Royal Highness and a Princess of the House of Saxe-Hildbourg-hausen.' But Hildbourghausen was not required. He really was there at last.

His decision taken and accepted he was the old Duke again, putting a good face on it, and even pleased to be taking a bride younger than his oldest child. He said to Lady Harcourt, 'My daughters once happily & respectably settled, I do look forward with every fair prospect of happiness, considering the high character the Princess Adelaide bears & the insight that her letters give me into her mind & resolution not to be dazzled by the offer, but seriously reflect on the step which she means to take.'

The Queen had heard of the 'reputation for amiability' of Princess Adelaide of Saxe-Meiningen, and it was on her sugges-tion that the match was made. Adelaide was a thin, shy, retiring girl of twenty-five who had been carefully brought up by a widowed mother. Her vapidity could have destined her for spinsterhood, and she was bound to seize on the opportunity of a husband, especially one with the strong possibility of transforming her from a minor Princess to a Queen – it would be so good for Saxe-Meiningen. It was politics alone that brought Adelaide to William. There was no added financial attraction. Like the brides of the other two brothers, she came without a dowry.

With the difficult Clarence at last disposed of, the Prince Regent could bring his brothers' marriages together before Parliament, thus dealing with Cambridge's complaints. He slung them together into one Royal Message adding for good measure a request on behalf of Cumberland. Cumberland had not received a grant at his marriage four years earlier, and the Regent wanted this omis-sion redressed.

Making up the bill he was to send to Parliament presented problems. Clarence, still smarting from his treatment over Miss Wykeham, asked for an impossibly large increase in allowances, for all his debts to be paid and for substantial provisions to be made for each of nine surviving natural children. As far as he was concerned, if the nation demanded he should give it an heir, then the nation could damn well pay. For all his bluster, once again he could not stand his ground. But the Royal Message did go forward with a request for him to be given a grant greater than those of his younger brothers.

There were difficulties too with his ministers, Liverpool and Castlereagh, who had the thankless task of putting the Bill before Parliament. To them, Royalty did not seem to appreciate that the vast demands they made might prove a little unpopular. Already this large family was costing £1 million annually in allowances. The debates had to be held back for a day while they persuaded the Regent to reconsider and make out a more moderate request.

Even so the Bill presented on 15 April by Lord Liverpool to the House of Lords and Castlereagh in the House of Commons was not likely to pacify the Radical opposition. An annual increase in grant of £19,500 for Clarence, and £12,000 for Cambridge, Cumberland and Kent (in the event of his engagement being announced), plus an equivalent sum as an 'outfit' to help each marriage set up, made a grand total of £110,000 to be extracted from the public's pockets. In 1818, beyond Windsor and Claremont and Bushey, Britain was still suffering from the slump. A correspondent to America wrote:

The Northern Sentinel, Burlington, Vermont, published on 17 January 1818:

'. . . the conclusion universally adopted here is that we are not very remote from some great convulsion . . . there is nothing else but railing in poetry and prose'.

As one MP was to point out, this vast demand was being added to the budget at a time when there was a bill in progress to 'deprive the widows of officers even of their pensions, if elsewhere they could obtain a pittance for their support' – the Treasury like everyone else was desperate.

The Prince Regent's bill also had the misfortune of being put to Parliament by a Tory Government that was utterly undistinguished, while the Opposition was lively, sharp, and longing for the opportunity to attack the Royal Family and the Royal Marriages Act. As Wellington was to comment,

> 'The Royal Dukes are the damndest millstone about the necks of any government that can be imagined. They have insulted *personally* two-thirds of the gentlemen of England and how can it be wondered at that they take their revenge upon them when they get into the House of Commons? It is their only opportunity, and I think, by God! they are quite right to use it.'

Castlereagh opened the debate in the Commons, presenting the unwelcome demand in such a low-key manner that he was practically inaudible. Since his diplomatic triumphs in the Napoleonic Wars he had sunk to such a degree of unpopularity that he could not afford to walk the streets for fear of mobs assailing him. 'To excite some of the members of the Royal Family to marriage was now an object of much importance to the country,' he said, and it was clear that the excitements would have to be financial rather than sexual. But as his speech went on the financial demands got less and less, in an attempt to placate a dissatisfied House. 'It is indispensably necessary that the Duke of Clarence, to maintain the splendour of his station, be granted an increase of £12,000 – or at the very least, £10,000.' Eventually he stuck at £6000.

The Tory point of view had also been put in the Lords by Liverpool, scrupulously backed by historical precedents. At all events the status quo must be maintained, the Royal Dukes must be permitted to 'live in a manner corresponding with the rank to which it had been the will of Providence that they should be born'. However bad things were, they must be kept the same, because if they were not the same, they would only be worse; such was Lord Liverpool's philosophy. He was the 'arch-mediocrity', an unprepossessing, uninspired, work-a-day Prime Minister.

From the opposition benches came one of the sharpest politicians of the age, the Marquess of Buckingham. He led the attack with: 'The splendour of the Crown is intimately connected with that of the subject . . . the feelings of the Crown ought to be in unison with the feelings of those over whom it presides; the moment they ceases to be, nothing can remain to the people but submission to power and despair of redress' – and, implicitly, recourse to revolution. 'Surely it is not too much to hope, that the splendour of the Crown can be maintained without a further diminution of the few remaining comforts of the people . . . it is not too much to expect, that every means will be resorted to before any resort is had to new and oppressive taxation.'

The Radicals had a slogan for their attack: *economy*. 'In the spirit of the times, and the temper of men's minds, there is growing more and more, a determination, deep-rooted, fixed and immoveable, that the people will have economy,' said Lord Brougham, the energetic, voluble champion of the opposition in the Commons. 'I prefer a monarchy, with all its trappings, to a republic; but on the condition that they be cut down to the lowest amount.' The radicals kept the prospect of revolution up their sleeves while putting their faith in this novel panacea. 'Up to this moment, economy has never been acted upon.' 'The plan of gross extravagance in contemplation' was a fatal step in the wrong direction. 'The royal dukes, in common with every other description of person in the country, must yield to the pressure of the times.'

It was suggested the marriage grants come not out of the pockets of the people, but out of the Privy Purse, the £60,000 allotted to the mad King. Mr Tierney totted up the money going to Windsor.

'It could not cost more than £18,000 a year to maintain the health of an aged lunatic; there was £170,000 a year from the royal estates; there was a grant of £58,000 for the Windsor establishment. If the Noble Lord (that is, Castlereagh) means to say that Her Majesty and her two daughters, together with the King cannot be maintained on *less* than this sum, I am ready to debate the matter any day he has to spare.'

But this line of attack was felt to be underhand. The one complaint all parties could join in was against the Royal Marriages Act that had helped bring about the present situation. Sheer indig-

nation at George III's 'extraordinary and unwarrantable inno-
vation' was expressed everywhere. It offended patriotism: 'It is not
for Great Britain to portion its princes according to any scale of
advantage they might derive from any petty principality in
Germany' and it offended morality, as Wilberforce expressed with
his customary dignity:

> 'It precludes the dukes from entertaining the best feelings,
> and from forming the connections which would at once
> promote their happiness and guarantee their virtue. It seems to
> imply, that they could be rendered better political characters by
> being worse men, which is one of the most mistaken notions,
> as well as the most immoral of public doctrines.'

But if the Commons could not attack the Regent who upheld
the Royal Marriages Act, they could at least discuss and compare
his brothers whose fortunes were now in their power. Speaker
after speaker would stand and begin that 'there was not a warmer
friend to the House of Brunswick in three kingdoms than himself',
but . . . Kent came off best; he was a friend to the Radicals, it was
considered that he had made reasonable efforts to pay off his debts,
and 'his public conduct entitled him to the just esteem of all who
knew him'. The House was more than ready to grant him something. Cambridge also found approval for 'the uniform tenour of
his conduct'. But as to the hated reactionary Cumberland, MPs
could not decide which they would rather authorise – a grant to
him or his immoral wife – and ended up giving £6000 to the
latter, by a narrow majority of seven votes.

By this time the Radicals had got the sums under discussion
down to an increased grant of £6000 each and a corresponding
outfit. But Clarence was not even to have this; there was no love
for him in Parliament. Mr Canning tried to set forth his self-
sacrifice in marrying:

> 'His Royal Highness would not have thought of contracting
> this marriage, it would never have entered into his contem-
> plation to engage in this alliance, if it had not been pressed upon
> him as an act of public duty. Into this alliance His Royal

Highness entered, not for his own private desire or gratification, but because it was pressed on him for the purpose of providing a succession to the throne.'

The House burst out laughing. 'As the professed object of the present measure is to enable the royal duke to support a greater splendour,' said Mr Sumner, moving that Clarence's increase be reduced to £3000 plus £3000 outfit, 'it ought first to be ascertained, that the sum will be made available to the purpose. But if public report speaks truly, the Duke of Clarence is greatly in debt' – up to £80,000. 'It will be found that the House is actually throwing away the money . . . Because he has extravagantly thrown away that which Parliament has already granted him, are we to make good the effects of that extravagance?' Sumner's amendment was carried by nine votes.

The result was received with loud shouts of approbation; amidst which, Lord Castlereagh rose and observed, that 'since the House had thought proper to refuse the larger sum of the Duke of Clarence, he believed he might say that the negotiation for the marriage might be considered at an end'. The Duke sent a message to Parliament the next day, 'to declare with the utmost deference to the feelings of the House, that he felt himself compelled to decline availing himself of the provisions intended for him'. Injured dignity had won at last. So after all the hunting and the fuss the Duke of Clarence was to remain a bachelor.

★   ★   ★

A satire 'in the manner of La Fontaine' recorded the undignified progress of the Parliamentary grant-grabbing in the *Morning Chronicle*. Castlereagh starred as an 'ancient Donkey' come to fleece the sheep – the people.

> '*He told them of the King's intentions*
> *To get a score nephews and nieces*
> *And that he came to take dimensions*
> *Of their hindquarters and their fleeces* . . .
> *He trusted that his faithful flock*
> *Would feel a pride in being fleec'd,*'

But

> '*Although he did not bate a shilling*
> *Of his demands when first they met*
> *He soon appeared extremely willing*
> *To take whatever he could get.*'

The verses concluded with an exhortation to vote the Government out in the general election next year. But for the time being the put-upon populace had to content itself with watching the ludicrous antics of their superiors as they approached the blessed state of matrimony.

*   *   *

XI
Duty and Discomfort

Spring 1818

In the spring of 1818 Prince Leopold was looking exceedingly
pale. Still keenly affected by Charlotte's death, he remained in
melancholy mourning on £50,000 a year at Claremont.
Nevertheless, he managed to take some interest in the promotion
of his family – the House of Saxe-Coburg – into the ruling
English dynasty, and it was on his advice that the Duke of Kent
wrote to his younger sister, Princess Victoire, for a decisive answer
early in the year. Kent remained in agonies of discomfort over
the 'constant dissimulation' he was forced to make to Mme de St
Laurent. Victoire's assent, arriving on 6 February, still left the
problem of how to excuse himself from Brussels.

'My poor companion,' he wrote to a friend, 'has been more or
less constantly brooding over the chance of my marrying and it
has occasioned us both five weeks of more misery than language
can describe . . . she relies on the promise I was compelled to give
her that I would not go over to England, unless my friends, who
have the management of my affairs in their hands, state that my
coming over is *indispensable* to perform some *legal* act.'

The woman for whom Kent was abandoning his old companion
was described by Prince Leopold's aide, Baron Stockmar, as being
'of middle height, rather large, but with a good figure, with fine
brown eyes and hair, fresh and youthful, naturally friendly and
cheerful, altogether most charming and attractive . . . she dressed
well and in good taste'. She had married Emich Charles, Prince of
Leiningen, when she was only eighteen to his forty-one. It had
been a dull marriage to a dull man, but she had done her duty and
given him heirs – Charles Frederick William and Feodora. Since

his death in 1814, she had been Regent of his principality on behalf of her young son, ruling the little state from his pocket-palace in the village of Amorbach. She relinquished the freedom and authority of this post to marry a man who was unattractive, ageing, and in debt. Before Charlotte's death she had turned down the Duke's proposals, but now the lure of the most important throne in the world carried her to the altar again.

The Duke was also a reluctant bridegroom. He believed that somehow he could live in splendour without marrying to obtain an increased allowance. He had hoped that Clarence might marry or the Prince Regent might divorce so he could continue the pleasant existence in Brussels which he describes in a letter he sent to his friend (and secret sister-in-law) Mrs Fitzherbert in Brighton:

'I was received by the King, Queen, Prince of Orange [Charlotte's rejected suitor] and his young wife . . . I am asked to dine, or sup, with them whenever they have any public party, but this is rare, as the court live uncommonly retired by choice . . . in the new capital. Otherwise I accept no invitations, as there is such a mixture of company of all countries and politics in this place, that it would be quite impossible to discriminate; and I only invite occasionally four, but oftener two, friends to dinner, to have my rubber of whist at what evenings we don't go to the theatre . . .

'I continue to be an early riser, but not so early as I was at home, for I now rise at $\frac{1}{2}$ past 6, or $\frac{1}{4}$ before 7, instead of at 5 as I used to do; and I am seldom out of bed after 11 the theatre rarely being over later than 10, and all parties except amongst our countrymen, breaking up about the same hour. Thus . . . I am living most quietly . . . in the full spirit of my plan of economy and retrenchment. My house, though old, thanks to painting, papering, whitewashing, carpeting, and putting up a number of stoves, is very tolerably comfortable . . . with a fine flower garden and a good deal of fruit on the wall . . . and I have . . . my horses, equipage, and stablemen within my own yard . . .'

But the Duke of Kent was soon to leave this sanctuary: he was on unfriendly terms with his brothers and he was determined to do better than they. Also, he was firmly persuaded that he would be King. 'My brothers are not so strong as I am,' he often said. 'I have lived a regular life. I shall outlive them all; the crown will come to me and my children.' Only his older brothers, York and Clarence, stood between Kent and the Crown after the Regent.

But the Duke of Kent, soldier though he was, did not have the courage to tell his mistress that he was embarking on a plan to save his finances – and the throne of England. He wanted to avoid her nagging and her tears, but still keep his options open.

After the invitation arrived which pretended that the Duke was needed in London on legal business, the Duke wrote to his equerry and friend, Wetherall:

'. . . I communicated *your shewable* to my poor faithfull Partner, on Friday, the day it arrived (and for which she was certainly in a degree prepared by the preceding one of the same nature which you had written some time before). It was however but too evident, it shook her a good deal, and that she looks forward to the separation of two months, which she considers it will be (or rather of 10 weeks, for the plan settled between us is for me to stay over my sister Elizabeth's birthday on May 22 and that we should set out from here on the 14th March) as ominous of evil; indeed tho' she behaves admirably about it I see her tears floating down her Cheeks, and, at times . . . she lets out her fears, alarms & suspicions, and you may judge how my heart sinks within me & Bleeds at every mark of tenderness & affection she bestows on me; . . . there is that chance, if the secret is well kept, as I trust it will be, of my reverting to my present quiet & peaceable home with my beloved companion of eight & twenty years, & I must try to keep that hope alive in my Bosom, while we part. On the other hand, I feel I have a duty to render to my Country if my Elder B———r does not m———y, and if I am compelled to make the sacrifice of my poor companion, I hope Providence will turn it to her happiness & support us both thro' the arduous trial.'

Bad colds and hurricanes made travelling difficult, so the departures of the Duke and his lady were delayed till the 16th. '. . . she for Paris, I for England . . . I do hope, now the hurricane has ceased . . . that I shall be able to cross the Water on the 21st'.

The Duke escorted Madame to her carriage and watched her driven away towards Paris attended by one of his footmen. She thought she would see him at the beginning of the summer. He felt in his heart of hearts he would never see her again. He would soon be with the woman who was to be mother of his child.

The Duke arrived alone at his apartments in Kensington Palace on 22 March to plot his wedding. Although both Victoire and the Regent had agreed to the proposal, arrangements still had to be made with the Princess's trustees, the King of Bavaria and the Duke of Baden. The British Minister at Wurtemberg busied himself about southern Germany on his behalf. Meanwhile Parliament was debating his allowance in the event of marriage, and MPs found time to compliment Kent on his sympathetic views and the superiority of his character to those of his brothers.

Once these matters had been settled, Kent arranged to pay off the unhappy Madame. A document dated 8 May details an annual allowance with a substantial increase to come after 1822:

'. . . so that nothing, I hope, has been omitted to give the only solid proof that lies in my power of the affection I have for her and the great longing I have that in every way she will be in a position to undertake all she thinks will contribute to her comfort and well-being . . . May she find in all this the proof of how dear she will always be to me, and how much I want her to look on me, to my last breath, as a true and faithful friend in every eventuality.'

On 16 May, Kent set off for his German altar in his post-chaise, 'lately newly ornamented with E V – Edward and Victoire – painted on it, with coronet above, in green relievo'.

Victoire's mother, the Duchess Augusta of Saxe-Coburg-Saalfeld, who already had one son, Leopold, living in England was dubious about Victoire's match with the old Duke. On 26 January, she had written in her private diary: 'Dear, good child, she seems so unperturbed at what lies before her and this almost worries me . . . In a few months' time she may possibly become the wife of a man she hardly knows. If it is God's will that this union should take place may he watch over her, for the marriage is certainly not of her own seeking.'

After the Duke's arrival she wrote:

'We had only expected the Duke of Kent tomorrow, but hardly had we sat down to luncheon when a Courier arrived with the news that the Duke would follow in two hours. We waited with much curiosity and poor Victoire with a beating heart. She had only seen him once before. At 4 o'clock he arrived . . . At first the Duke, man of the world though he is, was somewhat embarrassed at suddenly breaking in on our large family circle. He is a fine man for his age, has a pleasant winning manner, and a good-humoured expression. His tall stature helps to give him an air of breeding, and he combines a simple soldierly manner with the refinement of a man of the world, which makes intercourse with him easy and pleasant.'

The habitué of the dinner table had managed to win the heart of his mother-in-law, at least – but then, he was more her age, being only nine years younger. Kent was twenty years older than his prospective bride.

No time was lost. The betrothal ceremony took place two days after his arrival at the Coburg Schloss, where the couple exchanged rings. This event was followed by a grand dinner and a tedious concert. Another two days passed and they were married, as the Duchess described in her diary:

'May 29th . . . Louise, Sophie and Spath [Louise was the Duchess's daughter-in-law, and the future mother of Prince Albert; Sophie was the Duchess's eldest daughter; and Spath was the lady-in-waiting] lunched with me, and at 8.30 we again drove "en cérémonie" to the Schloss. The Duke of Kent was already standing under a velvet canopy in the brilliantly lit Riesensall. He looked very well in his English Field-Marshall's uniform and Victoire charming, in a white dress trimmed with white roses and orange blossoms . . . A salute from the *Festung* proclaimed that the ceremony had been accomplished. We then returned to the State Rooms, after which, rather late, there was a State Dinner. I accompanied the newly married couple to their apartments, which had been charmingly prepared for them.'

Three days later the anxious mother wrote of her hope that 'the dear good child will find in this second marriage all the happiness which she had not quite attained in her last one . . .' and 'I hope Victoire will be happy with her really very amiable husband, who only in middle age, makes acquaintance with family life and will therefore perhaps appreciate it all the more.' She was ignoring the fact that he had just put twenty-eight years of domesticity behind him.

A Church of England wedding was also required, as the Lutheran service was insufficiently binding for a union that might produce a Crown Prince. Edward and Victoire set off without delay for England.

So the beginning of their acquaintance – and marriage – was spent in the discomfort of travel across Europe to Calais via Frankfurt and Brussels. Victoire was sad at leaving her two children. Charles had already left for Switzerland with his tutor, and Feodora was left behind in Coburg with her grandmother.

A report in *The Times* describes some of the journey:

'The Duke of Kent was the other day agreeably surprised by a reception at once pleasing and singular. On his entering the little town of Bisschosgeim (Tauberbischoffsheim) on the frontier of Leiningen, he was preceded by all the young girls, tastefully dressed in white, decorated with ribands and garlands of roses, who strewed flowers before his carriage, and expressed their gratitude to him for his kindness and condescension in passing through their little town. The Duke conversed for some time with principal inhabitants . . .'

The Royal yacht, having delivered one lot of newly-weds, was waiting at Calais to collect the next batch – this time the Kents.

On their arrival there at the end of June, they met the Duke's sister, Princess Elizabeth, and her bridegroom the Prince of Hesse-Homburg, now given the affectionate nickname 'Bluff'.

They had arrived on 'the most lovely day that ever was', which compensated Elizabeth for the pangs of parting from home and family. The eight weeks since Elizabeth's wedding had been spent first at the Royal Lodge at Windsor and on 3 June they left London for Brighton from where they would proceed to Dover '. . . whence they will embark for the Continent . . . if the shock of Elizabeth's departure should produce any ill effect upon the Queen, or if her Majesty's health should become worse, the Princess will return to town immediately. Her Royal Highness seemed to suffer the severest emotion on this first separation from her family and country . . .' wrote a correspondent in the *Gentleman's Magazine*.

Elizabeth had never before been separated from her sisters, her mother or England, and she was delighted by the receptions and parties at foreign courts on the way to Homburg. After a reception at Schaumberg, the Princess wrote to the Regent asking him to send her a miniature of himself for her to hang around her neck. Even the odious but dazzling Duchess of Cumberland was wearing one of her brother-in-law. She went on to say:

'In England we have no idea of the magnificence of the dress on the Continent, particularly pearls, which they have in enormous quantities, all hanging about them, but the instant dinner is over they undress, and then look horrid.

'. . . the day I went to pay my respects to the Empress of Russia I shall never forget the scene of bustle and confusion I was in; the Dss of C————d doing the honours to perfection, but from eleven in the morning till nine at night the room was full. I must make You laugh at her asking me, with my ugly figure, to put on one of her gowns. I could not help saying: 'Do look at Your beautiful figure and look at mine. You mean it kind, but thank God I am not a Fool.'

When the bridal couple eventually arrived at the castle at Homburg, the homesick Elizabeth found to her delight that portraits of her father and mother in their Coronation robes had been hung in her apartments. Her Bluff had demonstrated a hidden romantic side by secretly buying them in London and having them sent on ahead.

The castle, Elizabeth's new home, was rather crowded as many relatives were living in it. Life revolved around meals, and she became even larger. Her sister Augusta later described a visit there.

'I found Her very much altered at first; and had I not had Her picture previous to seeing Her, I should not have guessed it was Her . . . by degrees I have quite retraced Her features and countenance. She is very large and bulky. Her face is very broad and fat, which makes Her features appear quite small and distended. But what strikes the most is, that not wearing the least bit of Corset, Her Stomach and Her Hips are something quite extraordinary. Her face is *not at all old* and though she commonly has to drive at a foot's pace, she is very active in the House. She goes out every day, the whole winter through, in Her open Carriage; and generally by Herself, reading all the while. She is uncommonly cheerful; and I may say has every reason to be as perfectly happy as she appears to be. She is universally respected by the whole Country; and the good she does is incalculable.'

Augusta went on to describe Elizabeth's life in the dilapidated castle of Homburg:

'One day very much resembles another. This is the ordinary routine. At seven the drum beats a reveille; a few minutes afterwards the stoves are lighted. At half past eight the servant brings hot water, and at nine coffee, hot milk, a small white loaf, a piece of brown bread, a slice of butter, a salt-cellar, and in a saucer ten small lumps of sugar. At half-past eleven a message from the Princess to know how I have slept, and if I should like to go out with her at a quarter or half-past twelve. At which hour, if it is tolerably fine, we go out in a drosky, and afterwards walk, returning home by a quarter before two, when the trumpet sounds for dress. At two it sounds again to serve up dinner. I then go through a long passage, down twenty-five steps, and up twenty-five steps, which leads me to another long passage, and that to the drawing-room, where I find two or three more guests. The door opens, and the gentleman esteemed the most considerable gives me his arm. We walk into the dining-room, and stand still till the other door is thrown open, when the grand maître d'hotel, with a white wand and hat in hand, enters, preceding the Landgrave and Landgravine, followed by the aide-de-camp of the former and the maids of honour of the latter. All sit down to table, the Landgrave having made me a sign to sit down beside him on his left hand . . . Three or four times in the week the band plays during dinner, after which the brother gives his arm to the princess and the prince his arm to me. During all these movements the ladies curtsey and the gentlemen bow down to the ground. We walk into the drawing room, the prince and his brother stand at one window, the princess and the ladies sit near another; the gentlemen stand at the other end of the room, unless any one happens to be addressed by the prince. Coffee is served, after which the prince and the princess leave the room, making bows and curtsies, which are answered by profound bows from all present. A maid of honour throws a shawl over the princess's shoulders and walks after her, first turning to salute the company. The aide-de-camp does the same and follows the prince, after which everybody retires. The drum beats soon after as a salute to the prince and princess as they drive out in a drosky, returning before six. About half-past six the princess sends for me. A servant with a lantern lights me downstairs to her apartments, and I sit with her in her boudoir till eight o'clock strikes. The servant then lights me through the passages and up the twenty-five steps, and I arrive at the drawing room, where I find a maid of honour at the tea-table, and about a quarter of an hour later the door flies open and the prince and princess enter. The former takes his tea, and then desires the card-parties to be formed, he playing at one table and the princess at another. At a quarter before nine the other door opens and Prince Ferdinand, the Landgrave's youngest brother, comes in and bows to the company. He walks up and down and looks at the players at a little distance, then sits down, and then walks again. I sit at the corner of the prince's table. A few minutes after the drum beats for some time. At half-past nine the aide-de-camp and a captain, who is always in waiting, come in with low bows, and almost immediately afterwards a servant enters, goes up to the grand maître, and announces supper. He is probably playing at the prince's table, but as soon as the game will permit he rises, takes his white wand and hat from the chair on which he had deposited them, and comes up to the princess's table, where he stands till he catches her eye. He then announces supper, makes a bow, and retires. As soon as the parties break up, all go to supper, as before to dinner. The prince and the princess retire as soon as it is over, so do the company, and a crowd of servants and kitchenmaids rush in to put out the lights and carry away the plates and dishes. The guard is relieved every two hours, at one, three, five, &c. At eleven at night a man blows a horn eleven times, once at one, and three times at three. On Sundays we dine at three, the Princes and officers all in full-dress uniforms, and company, to the number of thirty to thirty-five, all full dressed. On Mondays and Thursdays, the days for hunting, we dine at half-past two.'

*   *   *

XII
Converging Paths
May 1818

The Royal yacht, the *Royal Sovereign*, made another matrimonial crossing from Calais to Dover on Monday, 25 May. The Duke and Duchess of Cambridge arrived in England, three weeks after their German marriage, accompanied by her father, the Landgrave of Hesse, under a salute from the battery of guns on shore. It was a beautiful, peaceful evening and the crowd cheered loudly when they saw the Duke, who was supporting the Duchess in his arms. She was so seasick – the Channel had been tumultuously rough for so many German Royal brides and bridegrooms – that she could not walk unsupported. She felt so ill that she leaned heavily on the soothing arms of her new and adoring husband. She could hardly smile, but managed a faint nod to express appreciation to the cheering crowd and her new land. The Duke wrote to the Regent later that night: 'The Duchess has been dreadfully sick.'

The following evening they had driven the eighty miles from Dover and arrived in London. The old Landgrave of Hesse-Cassel followed behind them in a separate carriage.

The newspapers – and the public – were pleased with the match of the most likeable and respectable of the Royal brothers with this pretty Princess. Greville wrote: 'The Duchess of Cambridge has been received in a most flattering manner here, and it is said that the Duchess of Cumberland (who had arrived earlier) is severely mortified at the contrast between her reception and that of her sister-in-law.'

The Queen still refused to receive the Duchess of Cumberland but on the Thursday night after her arrival the Queen received 'the Duchess of Cambridge most graciously and affectionately'. Afterwards the couple went to Carlton House to one of the Regent's sumptuous suppers.

On Monday, 1 June, exactly a week after the bridal pair had been saluted by guns at Dover, they were married according to the forms of the Church of England in the Queen's drawing-room at Buckingham House. Once again the Archbishop of Canterbury performed the ceremony which was witnessed by 'different branches of the Royal Family, the Ministers . . . and others of distinction . . .' A newspaper correspondent described the new Duchess: 'She appears to be about 22 or 23 years of age, five feet six or seven inches in height, and of a most elegant figure; her countenance prepossessive, with dark eyes and hair. The Land-grave father of the Duchess, is a venerable old gentleman, about seventy, with a countenance the picture of good-nature . . .' The day after the wedding the Landgrave returned to Hesse-Cassel.

Londoners were thrilled to have a newly married Royal couple and the first Sunday after their wedding they were mobbed at Hyde Park. The new Duchess of Cambridge was 'so terrified by the presence of the mob that she nearly fainted away'. 'Her mildly expressive and interesting countenance and fine figure excited general admiration,' wrote the *Morning Chronicle*. She never took an active or stylish role in the Royal Family but she was a pleasant, albeit shy, wife.

The couple honeymooned at Cambridge Cottage on Kew Green, which after being occupied by the Clerk of Works was given to the Duke of Cambridge in 1806. Behind the cottages a mature and pretty garden led to a long paddock which joined the Royal kitchen and botanic gardens.

While she was still not received by the Queen, the Duchess of Cumberland stayed partly at Cumberland House on the Mall and partly at King's Cottage which the King had given her Duke in 1806. By chance, both the Cumberlands and the Cambridges were in residence in their neighbouring rural cottages during June. The couples were connected by the past. In 1798 the young Duke of Cambridge had asked his father for permission to marry his cousin, the woman who was now Duchess of Cumberland.

She was then only nineteen, but already a widow, with three children. First she accepted the Duke of Cambridge, then jilted him. Now she had divorced her second husband who was now dead and was married to her jilted ex-fiancé's brother, but through Cambridge's generosity a reconciliation took place between the Kew neighbours. But Cambridge's own kind heart could not sway his mother. Nothing could induce her to depart from her resolution not to receive the Duchess of Cumberland, although she was the daughter of her beloved brother. In vain were appeals addressed to the Queen by her relatives and crowned heads, including the King of Prussia.

The Queen's anger was inflamed by the behaviour of the newly married Cambridges. In June the Queen was so ill with spasms that her death was expected. 'Her illness,' wrote Greville, 'was occasioned by information which she received of the Duchess of Cumberland and the Duchess of Cambridge having met and embraced. This meeting took place as if by accident, but really by appointment in Kew Gardens; and the Duke of Cambridge himself informed the Queen of it. She was in such a rage that the spasm was brought on, and she was very near dying.'

The Queen still steadfastly refused to receive her daughter-in-law 'owing to unsatisfactory rumours about the Duchess's virtue', nor would she hear any pleas to change her mind. The Queen was so 'unwell' that her life was despaired of. The Prime Minister asked the Duke of Cumberland to leave the shores of England and to take his wife to Germany.

At this time the public was surprised to read in the papers that 'the Duke of Clarence was marrying after all'. Clarence was upset by the death of his son, Lieutenant Henry FitzClarence, in India. Marriage was a diversion from grief. He wrote to another son, George: '. . . had I a hundred children I could love them equally and you must know my heart *too well* to think I could forget those I have, I do, I shall and I must love.'

*   *   *

Kent had returned to England with his new wife at the end of June. On 2 July, the last of the Royal brides of 1818, Princess

[117]

Adelaide of Saxe-Meiningen, arrived with her mother the dowager Duchess. She came without a dowry and her trousseau was scant. Her family was poor. Her mother had agreed to accompany her daughter and to attend the wedding in England on the understanding that her travelling expenses were paid by the British government. She said that her duty as chief guardian to her son would not allow her to spend part of his estate in such a way. 'It is besides customary in Royal Families that the travelling expenses of the bride are defrayed by that Court to whose Royal Family the bridegroom belongs.' Lord Liverpool agreed to pay these expenses as he thought it expedient for the bride – probably the future Queen of England – to be chaperoned. Lord Keith whose daughter had spurned the Duke of Clarence's marriage proposal was now sent to escort the woman who had accepted his proposal.

As Princess Adelaide and her mother sped across Germany, the Duke of Clarence was nursing his grief for his dead son and the woman he was not allowed to marry. But Lady Williams Wynn spotted the Duke handing Adelaide's miniature around at a Royal concert just before she was due to arrive in England '... and bowing to each person when they passed it on, giving them credit for their approbation of his choice'.

Although committed to the marriage the Duke was not exactly eager to see his bride. He had replied to the Regent's secretary, Knighton, about the arrival of his bride '. . . sooner than eight o'clock it will be impossible for me to leave this lovely hospitable mansion though I am certainly most anxious to meet this Princess'.

The British government had provided the money for the trip, but they failed to provide any officials to greet the possible future Queen of England. There was no one to meet Adelaide and her mother when their coach arrived at the elegant Grillon's Hotel in Albemarle Street, London, except the hotel proprietor. A messenger galloped down to Carlton House. The young Princess nervously waited to see the unknown man she would have to go to bed with in the next week. There would be no chance to change her mind if she found him repellent on first meeting.

The Prince Regent finished his dinner and went up the road in his carriage to Grillon's Hotel to meet his future sister-in-law.

Later, in tremendous haste, a carriage and four horses raced along Piccadilly bearing the bachelor grandfather groom. Adelaide had this pleasant trait: she always tried to see the best in everyone, and this must have helped when meeting the Duke, who was over twice her age and twice her weight and size.

There was something tepid and meek about the twenty-five-year-old Princess, who was slight with light flaxen hair and pale eyebrows, which she never painted. Her father, who had ruled the tiny Duchy of Saxe-Meiningen, just north of Coburg, but had died when she was eleven, had held progressive and liberal ideas. A genteel education had taught her good morals and good needlework and in her home town her 'good works' were praised. She was plain but worthy. 'A small, well-bred, excellent little woman,' commented Lady Granville.

This Lutheran Princess was a contrast to the vivacious unpredictable and energetic Mrs Jordan; she accepted her future husband with his train of debts and bastards. She had been a good daughter and now she would be a dutiful wife.

The man Adelaide was to live with had been sent to sea by his father at the age of thirteen to promote confidence and pride in the Navy. He had not had the education given to his brothers. He was rough. He had served as Captain of the *Pegasus* and the *Andromeda*, and learnt nautical manners and speech that were unacceptable to aristocratic society. He spent fifteen-odd years of his life on the waves; but none of these years were during the Napoleonic wars when Britain was most in need of Naval defence. While his friend Nelson was making his name as a hero, he stayed at home with Mrs Jordan and his bastard children. The reason the nation did not use his services in these crucial times was that, though he clearly had an independent will of his own, he showed no sign of real intelligence. When he removed the ship under his command from the fleet in the West Indies, sailing it home to Plymouth across the Atlantic in mid-winter simply because he did not care for the Admiral above him who had replaced Nelson, it became clear that he was not of the calibre required to be a future Admiral himself. He did in fact eventually attain that post, but only in 1811 when the seas were safe enough to entrust to fools.

In the meantime the seadog had put down provisional roots at Bushey Park in Hertfordshire. He had alighted on Mrs Jordan after various short liaisons in his twenties. The only English-woman suitable for marriage at this stage was his dull first cousin, Princess Sophia-Matilda, and he did not care to seek abroad – Naval prejudices against foreigners had rubbed off on him. Mrs Jordan was one of the best-loved actresses on the London stage. She was described as 'brilliant and beautiful' but when the Duke pursued her in 1791 she was already thirty to his twenty-five and the mother of children by a variety of fathers. Her attraction was maternal rather than sensual, but Clarence pursued her so avidly it caused a degree of scandal.

Successful in his pursuit, he first set up house with her in his current residence at Petersham Lodge, and then, from 1797, at Bushey. Here they brought up the ten children that she bore him between her regular appearances on the stage. This life of 'blame-less irregularity' suited them both very well. 'Mrs Jordan is a very good creature, very domestic and careful of the children,' the Duke told a friend. 'To be sure, she is absurd sometimes, and has her humours. But there are such things more or less in all families.' In the role of devoted husband, he nursed her when sick; a letter has him apologising 'I have hitherto been prevented answering you by attending Mrs Jordan, who has been very ill indeed.'

The pleasant but unspectacular Bushey House, with its warm red brick and its spacious gardens, suited the Duke well, as he was not an outstandingly sociable person and found himself quite happy as a farmer. 'At this time of year, when the harvest is going on, one ought not to be absent a minute, except half an hour at breakfast and an hour to dinner. I am never out of the field the whole day.'

To be sure he would occasionally join his brother in carousing at Brighton, and he had apartments in St James's. Here he seems to have made an attempt to keep up the style of intrigue and secrecy for which the Prince of Wales was notorious, for when the rooms were redecorated he had had a door pushed through in the outer wall of the parlour beneath his bedroom. It was specially painted to look like bricks and he kept the only key.

But the mysteries of Clarence's life were few. He was basically unremarkable, though when required he rose to the occasion willingly enough. He celebrated his life at Bushey with a grand birthday party in 1806, to which all his brothers as well as much of the peerage and the military were invited. The house was decked out in bronze and imitation marble, and bands played on the lawn, while members of the public were allowed into the grounds to gaze from a respectful distance at the Royal banquet. The Prince of Wales led Mrs Jordan in to supper, and her children were brought into the drawing-room to be admired by all and sundry, while the band played excerpts from Haydn's *Oratorio of the Creation*. This last detail was much taken up in the satirical attacks made on the party by the Radical press.

But the general appearance of comfort and ease at Bushey rested on precarious foundations. The Duke's income was inadequate for the support of his ten bastard children, and though Mrs Jordan still had earnings from acting on the stage, long-standing debts from his early life overhung all efforts to make ends meet. He was sometimes driven to borrowing from Mrs Jordan, but as time went on it became clear that the only solution was her removal, to make way for a Royal marriage and the grant consequent upon it.

One night in 1811, Mrs Jordan's part in *The Devil to Pay* demanded that she burst out laughing, but instead, before an astonished audience, she burst into tears. Thus it became generally know that Clarence had decided they must separate.

'Could you believe, or the world believe,' she wrote to a friend, 'that we never had for twenty years the *semblance* of a *quarrel*? But this is so well known in our domestic circle that the astonishment is greater. Money, money, my good friend, or the *want* of it, I am convinced made HIM at the moment the most wretched of men, but having done wrong he does not like to retract. But with all his excellent qualities, his domestic *virtues*, his love for his *lovely* children, what must he not at this moment suffer?'

His virtues and qualities were perhaps best seen in the home; outside it, in politics, he played as he had in the Navy the role of a headstrong and foolish blunderer. His speeches in the House of

Lords appalled those he supported and delighted his enemies. The abolition of slavery drew remarks about 'these new-fangled principles of liberty, which have deluged Europe with blood . . . I assert that the promoters of the abolition are either fanatics or hypocrites and in one of those classes I rank Mr Wilberforce.' Known around Parliament as 'Billy Clarence', he was not generally taken very seriously, but neither was he much loved, and when he deserted Mrs Jordan and set off on his desperate pursuit of heiresses, he was for a long time publicly despised.

In choosing Adelaide for him, Queen Charlotte set the undistinguished buffoon that was her son in 1818 on the first steps towards becoming the comfortable and revered father figure later to be known as King William IV, the sailor king. At fifty-three it was a late start in life. But now the most important consideration was that this last achievement of the Queen be enacted before she died. Clarence and Adelaide could not wait to find out what they thought of each other. The wedding must take place at once.

★　　　★　　　★

XIII

It's Double your Money and Double your Fun

July 1818

It was a wonderful hot warm clear day (76°F), a good day for
Members of Parliament to win votes for the coming elections.
But alas, many of them had to join the caravan of Royal
relatives and other dignitaries and ministers along the King's Road
from St James's to Chiswick to visit the Dutch House at Kew.
Lord Sidmouth, Lord Liverpool, Lord Eldon, Prince Leopold, the
Duke and Duchess of Gloucester, the two spinster princesses,
Sophia and Augusta, the Duke of York and his untidy barren
wife, the Duke of Sussex without his left-handed wife, the newly-
wed Duke and Duchess of Cambridge – all made their way to
Kew for the great event: a double wedding.

The dying Queen had stopped for a few days at Kew to rest on
the arduous journey to Windsor, but now she was too ill to be
moved. The house was small and awkward for a Royal lodging,
but there was such a desperation to get the nuptials over of the
elderly bridegrooms, Kent and Clarence, that it was decided to
squeeze the ceremony into the Queen's drawing-room on the
first floor overlooking the Orangery and the botanic garden 'to
save time and money'. The haste was great as, if the Queen died,
the weddings would have to be postponed to make way for court
mourning.

But as with all Royal marriages, there was time enough for
sycophants to embellish the occasion. The Rector of Teversal's
efforts appeared in the *Gentleman's Magazine*:

'Again do Princely Nuptials greet the sight,
And Albion's realm around receives delight:
The Royal Dukes now take a blooming Bride.
May choicest Blessings o'er each Pair preside,
May joys supreme long on their union shine,
And Kings spring from the great illustrious Line!'

At exactly 3.30 p.m. the Dukes of Clarence and Kent were assembled ready for the double ceremony. They had the unprecedented honour in the history of the Royal family of being the only English Royal Princes to vow eternal fidelity together.

It was a bizarre wedding party; everything seemed wrong. The essential witness, the Queen, was nearly dead – in fact, the wedding had had to be postponed because of her illness. The cast was also extremely odd for this Royal performance: Kent, the Field Marshal who was not allowed to go to war, and Clarence, the Admiral who was not allowed to go to sea. The two German brides, Princess Victoire and Princess Adelaide, were bewildered; neither spoke a word of English.

Because of the laughter which had greeted the Prince of Hesse-Homburg four months earlier when he had promised his bride 'to lof her', the service was printed with German alongside the English, including 'Ich Will' – in case they missed the point – and phonetics were scribbled on the side.

It was appropriate that two of the valuable offshoots of the House of Hanover, Kent and Clarence, should be starting their reproductive cycle at Kew where the world's most valuable seedlings were nurtured in rarefied conditions. Exotic specimens, like the Strelitzia Reginae from the Cape of Good Hope, the Banksia from New South Wales and plants brought back from the tropics and semi-tropics by explorers were raised here. Kew was successful for uprooted plants – hopefully it would be successful for uprooted Princesses.

Across from the figgery, the vinery, the pinery, the peach house, the cherry house, the hot house, the rhododendron dell, the aviary, and the menagerie with its kangaroos, Algiers cows, a hog, and a fine blue nylghau from India, the Royal Family once again were getting ready to hear the familiar words of the wedding service as uttered by the Archbishop of Canterbury . . . 'to have and to hold, from this day forward, for richer for poorer, in sickness and in health . . .'

The drawing-room was fitted with a makeshift altar covered in red velvet for the occasion. Decked out with the 'valuable and magnificient' Royal communion plate, the whole arrangement succeeded in giving 'a most elegant and splendid appearance'. But it was not hard to see signs of the haste that lay behind the marriages.

The Queen had taken her seat beside the temporary altar overlooking her beloved garden after she had been wheeled in in her invalid chair from her bedroom across the hallway by the gouty Regent. Mother and son were not well. The Regent had been attacked by a mob crossing London two days before. 'The Prince Regent broke down in South Audley Street. A mob instantly collected as the carriage was known to be the Prince Regent's. The blinds were all drawn up, and he was concealed from their view; but they vociferated in a most indecent manner for him to show himself. At length HRH quitted the carriage, and made his way through the mews into Hereford Street, and took shelter in General Craddock's, followed and grossly insulted by the populace,' reported the *Morning Chronicle* on 13 July 1818.

The Duke of Clarence and his intended bride were introduced into the room, followed by the Duke and Duchess of Kent. They took their station at the temporary altar. Four red velvet cushions were before them – one for Adelaide and one for Victoire in the centre, and one on each side for the elderly grooms, both of whom had difficulty in kneeling.

The Archbishop of Canterbury and the Bishop of London with their assistants presented themselves to carry out this unique wedding service. Care had to be taken, it was joked, to marry the right brother to the right bride. But if the brides had got muddled up, would it have really mattered? Both Dukes had discarded cherished mistresses so they could enrich themselves with increased parliamentary allowances. And all Parliament wanted was an heir, so that it could continue its constitutional monarchy. The

Dukes were not marrying women – they were marrying wombs. They were not marrying for companionship, love or general progeny – all they wanted was one heir so England would not become a republic like France. There was also curiosity about the new Duchesses' powers of sexual arousal – which would have to be extraordinary to galvanise these fat quinquagenarians into copulation.

But although the aim of both the Dukes was the same, they were not friends, neither liked each other, and they were standing there as competitors, not brothers. At least they were at the starting line of the race together. At four o'clock the starters' flag went up and the ceremony began.

The competition between the brides was easily won by the new Duchess of Kent: it was remarked that she appeared buxom, bright and lively in contrast to the thin, pallid, wishy-washy Adelaide, whose features were spoiled by past scurvy. In costume, however, they were evenly matched. Victoire was dressed in gold and Adelaide in silver. Both dresses were trimmed with flounces of Brussels point lace and both had white satin lining their robes, diamond clasps at their waists and diamond coronets on their heads.

The two reluctant grooms stood in front of the altar: the soldier Duke's shiny bald pate, with its slightly absurd fringe of whiskers (newly dyed black for the occasion) rising loftily above the jaunty top-knot of his shorter brother's powdered Naval crop.

With the help of the German translations and phonetics, Kent married Victoire and Clarence married Adelaide and the British Royal Family was made a little more secure. Once the register of the Chapel Royal, St James, which had been transported for the occasion, had been signed by the newly-weds, the Regent, and the Queen, the Queen retired to her bedroom where she vomited. Weary and wan, the Queen was no longer the formidable prescence she had been three months earlier at the wedding of her daughter, Princess Elizabeth. 'The bloom of her ugliness is wearing off,' remarked one caustic commentator.

The rest of the party celebrated quietly at a dinner at five o'clock in the small dining-room downstairs. This party included many of the guests who had two years earlier seen Princess Charlotte marry Leopold, among them the Home Secretary, Lord Sidmouth, who had been present at Claremont during Charlotte's confinement and death, and, indeed, the widower himself.

That had been a romantic wedding, with a tragic outcome. The present affair was utterly unromantic. It was not personal hopes and fears that moved most of those present at the table. Who would father the next sovereign?

The Duke and Duchess of Kent were taken off after dinner, at 7.30, by Prince Leopold, who transported them in his travelling-chariot to Claremont. The remaining company sauntered out of the Palace and made their way across the gardens in open carriages to the cottage near the Pagoda, about a mile to the west, now known as 'the Queen's Cottage', where tea was taken. At the end of the day the cannon fired a double Royal salute, the celebrations were over, and the Duke and Duchess of Clarence left in a new travelling-chariot and drove home to his bachelor apartments in St James's Palace. The Prince Regent visited them two days after the wedding and they were 'sitting by the fire exactly like Darby and Joan'.

While the Dukes of Clarence and Kent were celebrating the success of their dynastic marriages, their brother the Duke of Cumberland was making a forced departure from England with his unacceptable wife, as required by Lord Liverpool. From Dover, the Duke wrote to the Regent from the York Hotel on 2 July: 'I cannot leave my native shore . . . I arrived here at seven o'clock last night and am to be on board the packet in half an hour as the wind is tolerably fair. I hope to be at Calais by ten o'clock.'

The reception for the weddings was held two days afterwards on 15 July at Carlton House. Though announced on the invitations as 'a small party en frocs', over 600 guests arrived, and the traffic on the Mall was such that besides 'a numerous assemblage of Bow Street constables' a detachment of Life Guards had to be used to control it. The public thronged outside the gas-lit courtyard to gaze at the arrivals and cheer the newly-weds. A grand dinner was followed by a performance by the Hanoverian band of the Coldstream Guards. But the grandeur and expense of the evening did not impress one observer, W. H. Fremantle, to whom it was 'dull and heavy . . . There was a grand display of all the Royal Duchesses,' he wrote to the Marquis of Buckingham, 'one more ugly than another. I think the manners of the Duchess of Clarence the best; and the look of the Duchess of Kent . . .'

On 27 July, the City of London offered its congratulations to the two couples, a day full of speeches. The Lord Mayor addressed the Prince Regent and described the pleasure of the City at 'every occurrence which strengthened their reliance in the preservation and continuance of the inestimable blessings which they enjoyed under the auspicious government of the House of Hanover'. The Regent himself had strikingly failed to provide for such occurrences; no love was lost between him and the men of the City. To the City's greetings the Duchess of Kent replied in a prepared phonetic speech:–

'Ei hoeve tú regrett, biing *aes yiett* so littl cônversent in this Inglisch lênguetsch, uitsch obleitschës miy, tu seh, in *averi fiú words*, theat ei em môhst grêtful for yur congratuleschens end gud uishes, *end heili*, flatterd, bei yur allucheon, to mei brother . . .'

'All the Princes are delaying, from day to day, their departure abroad expecting and looking out for the plunder to arise from the Queen's death,' wrote the cynical Fremantle. But if Clarence and Kent were vultures they could not hover for very long. Adelaide's mother, the Duchess of Saxe-Meiningen, had been dispatched back to her native land the day after the double wedding. Her daughter and son-in-law intended to follow her. Clarence had refused the grant of £6000 that Parliament had offered him on his marriage as being insultingly small, and in Hanover he could live respectably for less. But the Duke of Cambridge did not want his brother living in the territory he ruled, and having discussed this with the Prince Regent, wrote to him in his characteristically mild manner; 'as it has been my object, throughout life to pursue an honest and straightforward line of conduct, and to prefer a frank avowal of my sentiments to any indirect exposure of them, I flatter myself that I shall not incur your displeasure, nor be deemed to act inconsistently nor inconsiderately, by communicating to the Duke of Clarence what has passed on this occasion.' But the Regent, perhaps equally anxious to help his boorish brother settle his debts, could not agree with Cambridge, and let Clarence take himself off to Hanover.

So the Clarences sailed back across the Channel on the vessel built for all these Royal voyages, the *Royal Sovereign*. The *Royal Sovereign* was probably the most luxurious ship in the world, a three-master, especially built for the monarchy of the greatest Naval power. The hull was encrusted with carved beams and the portholes looked like picture-frames. Cupids cavorted around the interior furnishings. The Captain was always a distinguished officer of good breeding, and the hand-picked crew were on orders to refrain from Naval vulgarity. The cellars stocked the finest French wines and champagnes and the chef was a man of international reputation. But, sad to say, all his haute cuisine, all the Moselle and Claret, and probably every other superb refinement of the floating masterpiece would all go for nought as the members of the Royal House of Hanover leaned over the gilded rails, cursing the choppy English Channel.

When the Clarences travelled they were accompanied by Dr Beattie, a physician, who recorded the routine of the newly-weds:

'He breakfasts in the morning at seven upon tea and a simple slice of dry toast,' he wrote. 'A hamper lunch would be eaten in the carriage. At night, arriving at the inn, HRH takes tea, and only green tea, of which a supply was brought from Ghent. However late the hour or potent the beverage, the infusion never interferes with HRH's rest. Such is the power of long habit. Sherry is his favourite, indeed his only wine. The only beverage in which he indulges an innocent freedom is barley water flavoured with lemon . . . HRH does everything by system. When prevented by the weather from indulging in outdoor exercise he uses the drawing-room as a substitute.'

When they arrived in Hanover, the Duke of Cambridge, not one to bear a grudge, sent a cavalry escort to meet his brother and bride at the frontier, and arranged for a battery of guns to salute them. But there still remained the problem of accommodating the new arrivals. Cambridge occupied both the grand palace of the viceroy and the position of Governor-General. It was difficult for Clarence to live in an inferior house to his younger brother and also to yield precedence to him. Eventually he and his wife went to live rent-free in the less grand *Furstenhof*, with its own supplies of wood, game and garden produce.

The Duke was dreadfully homesick in this home of his ancestors. He wrote long letters to his steward at Bushey forbidding any alterations to his beloved house and farm, and exchanging gossip about pig sales, the parrot's health, candles and soap for the servants, cheap linen and the weather. To his son George he wrote: 'Necessity and not inclination keeps me *here* till I can live without incurring fresh debt.'

But this his new wife was helping him accomplish. She was not only cleaning up his language and polishing his gruff manners, she was looking after his accounts and under her influence his debts were diminishing rapidly. 'You would be surprised at the Duke of Clarence if you were to see him,' wrote Lord Colchester, 'for his wife, it is said, has entirely reformed him; and instead of that *polisson* manner for which he used to be celebrated, he is now quiet and well-behaved . . .'

While Adelaide was educating Clarence in the responsibilities of a Duke, Kent was educating Victoire in the duties of a Duchess. With his love for the pomp of official visits, he insisted on taking his wife along 'to visit many of the most respectable institutions and principal manufacturers of the metropolis' where they were still staying in August. She was broken into public life by having to listen to his endless streams of verbosity in a language she could not understand. They visited the British and Foreign Society 'for the Education of the Labouring and Manufacturing Classes of Society of Every Religious Persuasion' – where the Duchess

dutifully inspected needlework – they went to Woolwich to see
the Government Arsenal and Laboratory, they inspected the
General Penitentiary for Convicts on Millbank. They were also
seen at Covent Garden and the Coburg Theatre, where the
Duchess was greeted with great enthusiasm by the audience and
the curtain lifted to reveal a tableau of Claremont prepared as a
surprise compliment to her. She was genuinely popular with her
bright and attentive manner, and her public favour helped to cast
a good light on her husband.

But though the Duke's trustees had advanced him enough cash
for the nuptials and their accompanying expenses, the two months
thus spent doing the rounds of London meant that he was more
in debt than ever. Marriage had turned out to be but a short-term
solution to this lifelong complaint. When he went to see his
mother the Queen, who though dying was still aware of his
problems, she told him to go back to Germany.

She did not want to be faced again with Parliament's suggestion
that she help her son out of her Privy Purse. Kent admitted later
that his mother was 'a person of the greatest possible firmness of
mind . . . nothing but her pressing me to come abroad could have
made me do so'. While he was welcome enough in the streets, at
court no one wanted to have the debtor hanging around. So,
covering their retreat with the excuse that they were needed at
Amorbach, the Kents hurried away before the creditors closed in
on them.

On 6 September, the *Royal Sovereign* carried them back to the
Continent. On their way to Amorbach, the Duke dallied to
attend parades and inspect barracks wherever they were available,
to the irritation of the Duke of Wellington, who he met with at
Cambray. Lytton Strachey takes up the story: 'Wellington
dubbed him the Corporal. "God damme!" he exclaimed to Mr
Creevey, "d'ye know what his sisters call him? By God! they call
him Joseph Surface!" At Valenciennes, where there was a review
and a great dinner, the Duchess arrived with an old and ugly
lady-in-waiting, and the Duke of Wellington found himself in a
difficulty. "Who the devil is to take out the maid of honour?" he
kept asking: but at last he thought of a solution. "Damme,

Fremantle, find out the mayor and let him do it." So the Mayor of Valenciennes was brought up for the purpose and – so we learn from Mr Creevey – "a capital figure he was". A few days later, at Brussels Mr Creevey himself had an unfortunate experience.

'A military school was to be inspected – before breakfast. The company assembled; everything was highly satisfactory; but the Duke of Kent continued for so long examining every detail and asking meticulous question after meticulous question, that Mr Creevey at last could bear it no longer, and whispered to his neighbour that he was damned hungry. The Duke of Wellington heard him, and was delighted. "I recommend you," he said, "whenever you start with the Royal Family in the morning, and particularly with *the Corporal*, always to breakfast first." He and his staff, it turned out, had taken that precaution, and the great man amused himself, while the stream of Royal inquiries poured on, by pointing at Mr Creevey from time to time with the remark, "Voilà le monsieur qui n'a pas déjeuné." '

One call the Duke did not make as he paraded about the Continent was on his cast-off companion, Mme de St Laurent, now trying to adjust to life alone after twenty-eight years. He had given her an adequate annual allowance: 'the knowledge . . . of her *tranquillity* and calmness of mind under her altered situation . . . is essentially necessary to enable me to feel *comfortable* in mine,' he wrote, but any re-encounter would cause too much of the discomfort Kent had always wished to avoid. But though cowardly he was not heartless; he wrote to one of Madame's companions:

'Although an intimacy now of eight months with the Duchess [this was in January 1819] has attached me *sincerely* to *her* in *every* point that regards the Countess of Montgenêt [i.e. Madame] we must never lose sight that our unexpected separation arose from the imperative duty I owed to obey the call of my family and my country to marry, and *not* from the least diminution in an attachment which had stood the test of twenty-eight years, and which, but for *that* circumstance, would unquestionably have kept up the connexion until it became the lot of one or other of us to be removed from this world.'

While he performed his imperative duty with Victoire, Madame spent her last years in quiet obscurity in Paris.

*　　　*　　　*

XIV
The Milan Commission

Summer 1818

A n heir would surely soon arrive to fill the gap caused by
Charlotte's death. Already four weddings had taken place
in four months. The only contester for the race who could
not yet take a bride was the Prince Regent. He had the greatest
handicap of all: 'the damned Princess of Wales'. While his brothers
either went themselves or sent emissaries to Germany to bring
back suitable brides, the Regent sent spies to Italy to bring back
sordid details of the life of the Princess of Wales so he could
divorce her with justification.

He could not have legal sex – if he was capable of sex at all –
until he had jumped the divorce hurdle. Only then could he
marry and have a child so the crown of England would pass
down directly, from King to son or grandson – as it had for the
last 110 years – and not from King to nephew or niece.

Finding London closed to her in 1814, Caroline had gone
abroad and wandered first in Europe, then in the East, then again
in Europe, growing more eccentric as her English suite deserted
her and was replaced by Italians. She cast aside any pretence at
respectability. Her public and private behaviour was so garish
now that it was thought that she had set out to embarrass the
Prince of Wales and so punish him for rejecting her. The Prince
sent out numerous spies to obtain evidence.

The Prince was collecting proof and he was comforted that
even if he could not actually divorce her he could prevent her
from ever returning to England or ever being Queen. The file
recounting her escapades and sexual diversions was now thick.
The Prince, with his exalted idea of Kingship, was appalled that,

when his mad father died, Caroline's name would be in the Liturgy and the church congregations of Britain would pray for her well-being. Prayer appealed to Caroline. She had now embraced religion – as well as sex.

After her pilgrimage to the Holy Land, when she rode into Jerusalem on an ass, the Princess had had herself painted as a penitent Magdalene with her eyes heavenward, naked to the waist, revealing her spreading and wrinkled fifty-year-old bosom.

The portrait was one of her many presents to her swarthy lover, Bartolomew Bergami. Bergami – or Pergami as he liked it spelt – was in his early thirties and claimed to come from an old family of physicians who had lost their money and position in society. He had been a quartermaster in a regiment of Hussars and served in the campaigns of 1812, 1813 and 1814. His abilities as a lover led to his rapid promotion from Signor to 'Le Baron' when she had raised him from being her valet de chambre to chamberlain.

Caroline was indeed obsessional about Bergami. She bought him a villa at Pesaro on Lake Como for which she paid £7500 before the costs of alteration. Lord Brougham, the Princess of Wales's legal adviser, sent his brother James to report about his client's life. From the 'Villa Vittoria' James Brougham wrote:

'. . . The house is more of a cottage than a palace, but she had added two large wings . . . the confusion of buildings makes it look worse . . . The establishment consists of Le Baron, Col. Olivieri (equerry), Col. Vassali, a brother of the Baron's (who is first equerry), a singer and his wife and William Austin [who was alleged to be her illegitimate child] who dine at her table – also a girl (Bergami's daughter, Victorine) of 5 years old. A sister of ye Baron's is her *Lady* in Waiting and *his mother* superintends the linen and sometimes dines . . . The establisht. consists of 80 people, 63 of whm live in the house. There are 48 horses the finest Arabians I ever saw – and all *good* . . . A ship with a captain and eight men. . . .

'The style of the whole thing is more hospitable and plentiful, than dignified elegant or even comfortable . . . They eat off the commonest white stone ware, and the bulk of the spoons and forks are her old English things, but all such things as candlesticks &c have the Baron's arms upon them!! His picture is in every room. The child . . . calls HER mamma!! . . . Everything is "Le Baron . . ."

'. . . HER DEBTS . . . It is astonishing they are not more . . .

'She thinks there are people hired to kill or poison her, and the kitchen is watched accordingly – two servants parade the hall all night, besides the guards on ye outside. Pistols, blunderbusses &c in my room, besides dogs &c. The whole police at Pesaro in her pay. There certainly have been some odd things taken place and enough to excite a little caution . . .

'None of the English ever come near her, even old friends pass the door . . . She is much mortified at this . . .

'. . . ye Baron. In fact they are to all appearances man and wife, never was anything so obvious. His room is close to hers, and his bedroom the only one in that part of ye house. The whole thing is apparent to every one, tho' perhaps there might be difficulty in proving the fact to find her guilty of high treason . . . Leopold never wrote to her *at all*.'

At least Caroline entertained international society. Stories about her abounded. Her arrival anywhere was conspicuous as she had now designed a new uniform for her gentlemen with a startling new livery of brightly embroidered coats and feathered hats. At Geneva she had appeared at a ball dressed as Venus 'or rather not dressed, further than the waist'; she had bounced into the private box of the widowed Margravine who was in mourning, at the Baden Opera, yelling with hilarity and displaying a freakish peasant head-dress decorated with spangles and fluttering ribbons; Lord Redesdale said, '. . . when a partie de chasse had been made for her, she appeared with half a pumpkin on her head,' explaining to the Grand Duke that it was the 'coolest sort of coiffure'. She liked dressing like a little girl and at Genoa wore a short pink and white frock showing her fat legs in pink top boots and above showing a large expanse of over-blown bosom.

Lady Bessborough who saw the Princess of Wales at a ball in

Milan hardly recognised her. 'I cannot tell you how sorry and ashamed I felt as an Englishwoman,' she told Granville Leveson Gower.

'In the room was a short, very fat elderly woman, with an extremely red face, in a girl's white frock looking dress, but with shoulder, back and neck quite low (disgustingly so) down to the middle of her stomach; very black hair (in fact, a wig) and eyebrows, which gave a fierce look, and a wreath of light pink roses on her head . . . I was staring at her from the oddity of her appearance, when suddenly she nodded and smiled at me, and not recollecting her, I was convinced she was mad, till William Bentinck (the British envoy), pushed me and said: "Do you not see the Princess of Wales nodding to you?" . . . I could not bear the sort of whispering and talking all round about the Principessa d'Inglhilterra.'

At the time of his brothers' marriages, more reports of this obscene parody of Royal demeanour came back to England through ambassadors and correspondents – as well as the paid spies – and the Prince Regent decided to quash Caroline once and for all. He asked the Lord Chancellor to appoint a Commission to set up an office in Milan and to go through Italy and take sworn statements about her conduct. Sir John Leach, a lawyer, set up the Milan Inquisition (which eventually cost over £30,000). He appointed as investigators a King's Counsel named Cooke, Mr Allan Powell, a solicitor, and Colonel Browne, a former cavalry officer who spoke fluent Italian.

On 8 August 1818, John Leach instructed Cooke, Browne and Powell to initiate the exposure of Caroline's libidinous life. 'By command of HRH . . . you are hereby authorised to proceed forwith to Milan, and from thence to all other places at your discretion for the purpose of making enquiries into the conduct of HRH . . . the Princess of Wales since she quitted England . . . you are to engage all such assistance either legal or otherwise . . .'

The evidence was copious, vulgar and quite damning. Accounts told of Caroline and Bergami 'caressing each other with their hands' in a boat on Lake Como. Elsewhere his hands had been observed on her naked breasts and thighs. He had been seen to 'present himself several times before her almost naked and then take indecent liberties'. He had been found tiptoeing out of her room 'with only his drawers on'. Mlle Demont, the Princess's femme de chambre, testified that Bergami was usually present at the Princess's toilet when she was naked to the waist and that she would hear her mistress's door being opened in the night. Another chambermaid, Barbara Kusler, reported that 'from the appearance of Baron Bergami's bed and the impressions made on it she had clearly perceived that more than one person had been laying on it, and she had found wet spots on the sheets which put beyond doubt what had been going on in the bed'.

Giuseppe Sacchi, the equerry, had discovered the pair asleep 'and having their respective hands upon one another. Her Royal Highness had her hand upon a particular part of Bergami and Bergami had his own upon that of Her Royal Highness . . . Once Bergami had his breeches loosened and the Princess's hand was upon that part.'

Vincenzo Gargiullo, captain of her private boat, described how Bergami was not only present at the Princess's bath, but even followed her to the water-closet; how he would be seen kissing her as she sat on his knee, and how he would excite her ribald laughter by stuffing his Grecian robe with cushions to appear pregnant.

For not content with mutual grossness, it appeared the Princess and Bergami had turned their court into an orgy. Sacchi described the balls they held as brothels where the manservants would seek out whores, retiring to couple with them 'according to their pleasure and will'. The servant Majocchi mentioned a mulatto from Jaffa named Mahomet who was hired to perform obscene dances before the Princess.

Andrea Veronese, head of a servants' bawdy house, testified that the Princess had 'heard of the enormous size of his machine and sent for him by courier'. Next day she hired him as her confectioner. She made 'him put his machine on a plate and it reached across being nearly two palms in length and as thick as a horse's'. He said he had had connexion with her and showed publicly 1000 francs which she gave him. He assented that her French woman had seen him in bed with her. Little boys used to joke about him and call him '*Il fottitore della Principessa*' (the fucker of the Princess).

Majocchi also described how the Princess and Bergami shared the same carriage and how he kept a bottle 'to make water in', in the carriage.

An innkeeper who gave evidence actually reported seeing the couple in the act of fornication one morning when they had left their bedroom door slightly ajar.

The Commission eventually reported that the 'cool, clear and correct manner' in which evidence had been given confirmed its veracity and that 'in our opinion' this great body of evidence established the fact of a 'continued adulterous intercourse' between Princess Caroline and Bergami.

The Prince of Wales was jubilant. He had the proof that he needed now to divorce Caroline so he could marry and beat his brothers at the heir-chase. All he had to do was to have a trial now – at last he was close to ridding himself 'of that vilest wretch'. The risk was that, as his political advisers pointed out, he might also end up losing his throne.

★   ★   ★

XV
The Queen No More
September/November 1818

The Royal yacht had another journey to perform in September
1818 – it returned Prince Leopold to the Continent to visit
his mother for seven months. On 5 October the Duchess
Augusta of Saxe-Coburg wrote:

'Leopold is here! I am infinitely glad to see him, but greatly
shocked at the great change in my pet . . . The dear face bears
the imprint of a deep sorrow . . . Oct. 6th It is delightful having
Leopold here. He breakfasted with me . . . as in the good old
days . . . Nov. 6th. Leopold has come into town today to spend
quietly the anniversary of his great loss . . . he looked very pale
and drawn and I could see how much he was suffering . . .
December 16th Leopold's birthday . . . he is so unhappy . . . all
feel depressed by his sorrow . . .'

So Leopold's sister, the new Duchess of Kent, returned home
to an atmosphere of maudlin misery. Her husband, the Duke of
Kent, had a more recent cause for mourning, though he cannot
have felt it as tragically as Leopold.

On 17 November, Queen Charlotte had died in the Dutch
House at Kew, aged seventy-four, clasping the hand of her
favourite son, the Prince Regent, For all her faults she would be
much missed by her children. Her favourite daughter, Elizabeth,
who had made such a desperate move to escape her in marrying
Humbug, wrote from her new home: 'You have often heard me
say "no one will thoroughly know the value of my mother till
they have lost her" . . . You, who know how I ever loved her . . .

may well conceive how very much I am afflicted. The blow *is deep* and the sorrow rankles at my heart . . .'

As for public grief, the *European Magazine* described how Britain was supposed to feel on this occasion:

'Again the "earthquake voice" of Death has echoed through the Palaces of Britain, and the sound of a Nation's pleasures is once again hushed in the desert silence of a Nation's mourning. Scarcely have twelve brief months glided by since our land was shrouded in a night-like darkness, when the DAUGHTER OF ENGLAND was consigned to her ancestral tomb; and now the portals of that regal Cemetery are again unclosed, to receive within its hallowed sanctuary the remains of ENGLAND'S QUEEN!'

Her entry into the 'hallowed sanctuary' deserved the *European Magazine*'s exclamation mark. At the funeral, her coffin ran on articulated wheels and was pulled by six Yeomen of the Guard who were hidden under a velvet pall. This necrological novelty appealed to observers. 'It was impossible not to approve . . . The solemn effect produced on the spectators by the view of an object so interesting, slowly advancing, apparently from a motion of its own, was as striking and affecting as it was mournfully magnificent.'

So the nation disposed of Queen Charlotte. She had given birth to fifteen Princes and Princesses and on the day of her death she had not a single grandchild, male or female, to sit on the throne of England. There had only been four Royal births in forty years – three stillbirths and that of the lamented Princess Charlotte. But the old Queen had been told before she died that two of the new brides were *enceinte*. The Royal Marriages Act would, after all, succeed in keeping the caste of royalty pure.

The lunatic King was not told of his wife's death, or the death of Charlotte, or the marriages of his sons. He was never told anything. He lived in total silence in the Lower Suite of Windsor Castle with windows overlooking the North Terrace and across to Eton. Here no one spoke. The sound of any voice, familiar or strange, threw the King into an agitation and frenzy which lasted for days and sometimes weeks. So he was attended with extreme care in deathly and complete silence. He was entirely blind. He had neither seen anyone nor heard the voice of anyone, let alone that of his twelve children or his wife for years. But he spoke endlessly to everyone in his mind – ministers, children, fictional characters. He played at his harpsichord pieces by Handel from memory, singing in a voice both sonorous and touching. He would sit at his harpsichord for three hours or more after which he may have yet another short conversation with the ghosts of his mind. Although he could not see the clock and no one ever spoke to him to tell him the time, the old King was driven by some instinct to do the same things at the same time every day. So the King lived on; in total darkness, in total silence, in total ignorance. *Vivat Rex!*

★　　　★　　　★

XVI
The End and the Beginning

Spring 1819

Back in England news of Royal pregnancies revived interest in the last Royal birth – the stillborn Coburg Prince, who had died with his mother, Princess Charlotte, at Claremont twelve months earlier.

The rumours still persisted. Because of the laws of libel in England, a book was published in America under the name of the Duke of Hamilton's sister, Lady Anne Hamilton, Lady-in-Waiting to the Princess of Wales – though she later disowned authorship and it was regarded as unreliable.

'Mrs Griffiths (Princess Charlotte's midwife) certainly knows more about the death of her late Royal mistress than she has yet thought proper to communicate . . . she confessed to a friend of ours that the Princess Charlotte had actually been poisoned, and related the way in which she found it. Mrs Griffiths stated that, "after giving Her Royal Highness some broth (not gruel) she became dreadfully convulsed; and, being struck with the peculiarity of the circumstance, she examined the cup from which Her Royal Highness had drunk. To her astonishment she there perceived a dark red sediment, upon tasting which, her tongue became blistered." Mrs Griffiths asked Dr Croft what he had administered to the Princess; but she received no satisfactory answer . . .'

The Dukes of Kent, Cambridge, Clarence and Cumberland

had almost earned their extra Parliamentary allowances by impregnating their respective wives. Their virility – as well as their fertility – was demonstrated to a curious public. If there wasn't an heir alive there was at least one in a duchess's womb.

At the beginning of October it was announced that the Duchess of Kent was *enceinte*, but the Duke of Kent still insisted that she accompanied him on a trip he had planned to visit her sister Julia in her Swiss retreat. It was late in the year and the roads were treacherous for horses and carriages but they visited 'the glaciers of the Grindelwald' and went to 'the valley of the Lauterbourg to view the Staubbach'.

While it seemed not to occur to the Duke that there was such a thing as a miscarriage, he was most concerned to see that *his* child should be expertly delivered, and delivered in the right place. In this concern he was not alone. As early as 29 August 1818, the Prime Minister, Lord Liverpool, was writing to the Chancellor, Lord Eldon, about witnesses for the Royal births:

> 'It appears to me that it can by no means be necessary that the Duchess of Cambridge should return to England for her confinement. It would be most severe burden upon the Royal Family in general to oblige them not only to come over to England to be remarried, but to be compelled to return here on every occasion of the nature referred to . . . I think at the same time, if it can be done without inconvenience, it would be *adviseable* that some British subject should be in the house at the time of delivery, in order to insure testimony of the fact, if it should be necessary hereafter . . .'

The Teutonic ties of the English Royal Family were emphasised not only by the fact that the three brides and the one bridegroom in the matrimonial rush of 1818 were German, but that all four newly-weds were now living in Germany. It looked as if the future sovereign of England would be born in Germany. The Duke of Cambridge attended to his young wife's needs during her pregnancy in the quiet, steady comfort of his palace in Hanover. His brother, the Duke of Cumberland, was meanwhile in Berlin awaiting the second accouchement of his forty-year-old wife. Their first child had been stillborn in 1816. The Duke of Clarence was also still economising by living in Hanover. He had announced on 14 August that he meant to return to England within a few months, 'as he had the well-grounded prospect of her RH bringing him a Prince or Princess and it was their mutual wish that the birth should take place in England'. But as Lord Liverpool's letter makes clear, it was not the wish of the Government, and the return did not take place.

The Duke of Kent, though, was stubborn. He was determined that his child should first see the light of day in England. 'My wish,' as he put it to a friend, 'is that the *event* may take place on the 4th June (1819) as that is the birthday of my revered father; and that the child, too, may like him, be BRITON-BORN.' All his sense of pride and his frustrated ambition to serve the country were clearly strong. But, once again, he had more debts.

It was the same old story. He had spent too much on his trip to Switzerland. And strangely enough the 'little Elysium' he had made of his house in Brussels proved impossible to sublet. But with his aristocratic disdain for the lessons of cause and effect, the Duke borrowed £10,000 more to bring the dowdy little palace at Amorbach up to his exacting standards of comfort and refinement. Modernisations were carried out by specially imported English workmen and, of course, improvements were made to the stables so they would be fit for the Duke's horses. Many workmen were unpaid; so were suppliers.

The Duke of Kent was determined to get back to England where he would arrange ideal Royal obstetric conditions, and have the necessary witnesses. He wrote again to the Regent explaining that he wanted to come to England because in Amorbach there was 'a total want of convenience', and it would be cheaper for the Duchess to give birth in Kensington Palace than in Brussels . . . 'I have . . . made my arrangements to arrive at Calais on the 18th April . . .' But these reasons did not impress the Regent who had been antipathetic to Kent and his plans for years. Why on earth should the Regent or the Government pay for Kent to return to Kensington Palace? Why should the Royal yacht be put at his disposal?

The Regent wrote that Kent could not expect 'a cordial reception' on returning to England. Kent wrote to his friends detailing his complaints against his brother which he did not wish to be concealed from the world'.

Kent did not have enough money for the journey back to Kensington so he wrote a begging letter to his old friend, Lord Dundas. He made miserable noises about the dreadful notion that his child might 'first see light in a retired spot in Germany' and thus have to face 'the thousand-and-one rumours that might hereafter be raised relative to its (the child's) identity'.

This might seem absurd, as the Prime Minister's letter had clearly provided for the introduction of Government witnesses if Royal births took place in Germany. But Kent, with his hopes to provide an heir to the throne, was thinking back to 1688. Then the baby proclaimed as heir to the hated Catholic King James II had been strongly rumoured to be the child of a servant, smuggled into the Queen's bedchamber in a warming-pan. This rumour was generally accepted by the public who could believe anything of their monarch after four disastrous years of misrule. William of Orange arrived in England with his army because he said James II was trying to push an impostor prince on to the throne. In fact, in 1688, there were ample witnesses to the event but they were all considered suspect as the critical Archbishop of Canterbury had just been imprisoned. The Duke of Kent was determined that the Hanover Coburgs should not, like the Stuarts, end up as a dynasty in exile.

As for his debts, his old friends Lords Dundas and Fitzwilliam lent Kent £5000, enabling him to pay his most pressing bills in Amorbach and pay the cost of the 400-mile journey to England.

Although there was now money for the journey, the Duke of Kent still wanted to impress upon his family the importance of his future child's birth. He wrote to his sister, Princess Mary, Duchess of Gloucester, asking her to ask the Regent to provide the *Royal Sovereign* for yet another Channel crossing. He owed it as a duty to 'dearest Victoire'; but he added threateningly, 'if that cannot be managed I shall bring her over in the Packet'. These self-righteous demands irritated the Royal Family. 'I am outrageous with Edward,' wrote another sister, Princess Augusta, 'for he is behaving like a fool and a madman.'

But Kent got his way. The Regent unctuously communicated that he fully participated 'in the most anxious feeling for the safety of the Duchess on so critical occasion', but regretted 'that Your Royal Highness should have judged it expedient for Her Royal Highness to undertake a journey at her advanced period'.

But he went on to say that the *Royal Sovereign* was at the Duke and Duchess's disposal.

Crammed to the roof with people and luggage, their large shabby coach was driven by the Duke himself when they finally left Amorbach on 26 March 1819. The reason why he drove the coach himself was that he would not let his wife be driven by anyone else – but it was said to be to save the expense of paying a coachman.

Huge black trunks, the Duke's mahogany case full of crystal flasks and silver-mounted first-aid equipment, cages of pet song-birds, and lap-dogs were amongst the luggage. But the most important traveller was the midwife, Frau Siebold, who was also a qualified gynaecologist. Her qualifications were outstanding and unusual for those days. Also in the party were the usual servants, and the frail and beautiful Princess Feodora with her governess, Louise Lehzen, a Lutheran pastor's daughter.

Rumbling over the bad roads of the Rhineland on the long damp journey to England, the party presented 'an unbelievably odd cavalcade' to eye-witnesses. They made the journey 'by short day stages with their own horses as far as Brussels . . .' staying in cheap inns.

The first legitimate grandson to George III was born on 26 March, the same day that the Kents left Amorbach. In Hanover the Duke of Cambridge sent for his brother Clarence to act as official witness to this significant event. Clarence was received 'in full form' as befitted the proxy to the Regent, and accompanied by two elderly servants from his retinue, hastened to close off all access to the Duchess's bedroom. They then positioned themselves in an immediately adjoining dressing-room from which they could watch all that took place.

The moment the child was born Clarence rushed into the room 'to determine its sex by actual inspection', and then swept out again to dispatch couriers to London announcing the birth of a boy. The child was named George after his great-great-great-great grandfather, his great-great-great grandfather, his great-great grandfather, his grandfather and his uncle. Now he would share their name and one day he might inherit their throne.

George of Cambridge was – for now – the winner of the race, the heir to the three kingdoms. Cannons fired and Parliament sighed with relief. But although the Duke of Cambridge had won the Royal reproduction race and fathered the first child, his victory could still be snatched away if one of his elder brothers, Clarence or Kent, produced a live child. And in those days infant mortality was high.

But just as the Duke of Clarence and the Duke of Cambridge were celebrating the birth of the first member of a new Royal generation, the Duke of Clarence had to hurry from his brother's palace. He had news that Adelaide had gone into premature labour. Clarence was not nervous; after all he had been present at the ten births of his ten illegitimate children. But it was twenty-seven-year-old Adelaide's first confinement. She had recently contracted pleurisy after a cold, was bled and was in low health. Weakness and worry led to a premature labour. The day after little George of Cambridge was born, the Duchess of Clarence gave birth to an underweight daughter. This new heir presumptive pushed its cousin George Cambridge from the succession as Clarence was the elder brother. But only for an anxious seven hours. The poor little baby was not a competitor for the throne of England – she died on the day she was born. She had stayed alive just long enough to be baptised by the Duke of Cambridge's chaplain and christened Charlotte Augusta Lousia. She was buried beside the body of King George I in the crypt of the palace of Hanover.

So, for the time being, tiny little Prince George of Cambridge was still heir.

The news of this birth and death received during his journey north must have been a relief to the Duke of Kent. If the Clarence

child had lived all the plans made and debts incurred for his journey to Kensington Palace would have been worthless. For
Clarence was two years the older and the crown would only come
to Kent if Clarence had no children.

He sent his formal condolences and drove his pregnant Duchess
on and on to Calais. No threat now stood between Kent and the
throne of England. The man who was not even allowed to
govern the minute colony of Gibraltar would be King, after all.
He would be King and his son would be King. Huddled in his
huge coat, whip in hand, he hastened the horses – soon at an age
when most men are becoming grandfathers, he, Edward Duke of
Kent, was to be a father: the most important father in the world.

It was strange that Kent's three elder brothers never had offspring to block him from inheriting the crown and sceptre of
England. The Duchess of Cumberland was also pregnant – her
child was due eight weeks after the Kent birth. But as Cumberland
was six years younger than Kent his issue were irrelevant to
Kent's hopes and fears.

The journey to Calais of 400 miles took the Kents nearly a
month: they drove at snail's pace to safeguard against a miscarriage. The *Royal Sovereign* awaited them at Calais just as Kent had
wished. They crossed over in a high wind which made the sea
rough and the journey swift. Within four hours they were back
in England. The press briefly noted the arrival of the heir-bearing
party: 'His Royal Highness driving his own carriage, and at a
very slow pace, paying every attention to the situation of the
Duchess.'

From Dover the Kents went to Cobham where they were
entertained by Lord Darnley. The next day they arrived at
Kensington Palace where they moved into the Duke's old suite
of rooms plus some of the apartments which used to accommodate the Princess of Wales. The couple, sometimes seen
promenading in the gardens, began to excite sympathy and
interest. The pregnant Duchess seen leaning on the paternal arm
of her new husband made a happy picture for the much criticised
Royalty. Rubbing his hands, the Duke had a good word for his
wife: 'I trust my countrymen will duly appreciate the great

sacrifice and exertion made by her in travelling at a period drawing so near to her confinement,' he wrote, adding that he trusted his correspondent's prayers would be realised in witnessing 'a prosperous result to the Duchess's present interesting condition'.

Three weeks passed. As a final request to the Regent, the Duke of Kent wished to allay the 'thousand-and-one fears' for the child's identity that seemed to obsess him, by having official officers of state as witnesses at the birth of *his* child.

It was rumoured that when the Regent was presented with this request by Lord Liverpool he exploded. It was said that in his anger he announced he would boot the Kents out of the palace. But he relented. Kent once again had his way.

While the Kents waited in London, the Duchess of Cumberland was waiting in Hanover. (Her child born shortly after the Kents' was to be the blind King George of Hanover.) On 12 May a radiant Duke of Cambridge, his waiting well and truly over, wrote to his brother, the Regent, thanking him for being godfather and telling him:

'My son was christened yesterday . . . George William Frederick Charles . . . William acted as your proxy, and in consequence came in state . . . on this occasion, which had not occurred for 160 years, the ceremony should be performed with the greatest possible state . . .

'The Duchess and dear little George are both thank God remarkably well, and have not suffered in the least from the heat of the rooms which owing to the number of the people who attended and the mildness of the weather was very great . . .

'The Duchess of Clarence, who is now quite recovered, insisted upon being present at the christening, and she had such power over herself that she did not appear in the least affected at the ceremony. This shews the strength of her mind . . . for the scene must have been very trying to her feelings. She leaves Hanover on Monday next for Meiningen where she is to arrive on the 26th and from thence she goes with her mother to Liebenstein where she is to drink the waters . . .

'I was very sorry to hear, my dearest brother, that you have been suffering a good deal of late with the gout . . .'

On 24 May at 4.15 a.m. 'dear little George' lost his place in the succession. The Duchess of Kent gave birth to a girl 'as plump as a partridge'. The German midwife, Dr Siebold, assisted by Doctors Wilson and Davis, had delivered the new heir to the three kingdoms. The future Queen Victoria had been born just along the corridor from where the last King of England had died in the lavatory. The Royal Race had taken just eighteen months and sixteen days from start to the finish – from the time that the bells of St Paul's tolled for an hour to mourn the death of the future Queen to the time the cannon blasts echoed to mark the birth of the new Queen.

The Duke of Wellington and the Tory, George Canning, waited in the room outside until they were ushered in to testify that the child was that of the Duchess of Kent. Unable to control his excitement at siring the heir at the age of fifty-two, the Duke introduced the child to the assembled company as 'the future Queen of Great Britain and Ireland'.

This was anticipating things. His elder brother Clarence had a child a year later, who would have preceded Kent's; but she died after eight months. Also in 1820 the Regent's hated wife, and the dog-loving Duchess of York were to die, leaving their gouty widowers free to marry and reproduce if they were capable; but neither took the opportunity. Kent's intuition was right, he was father of a queen.

He expressed his thanks to God: 'As to the circumstances of the child not proving to be a son instead of a daughter, I feel it due to myself to declare that such sentiments are not in unison with my own; for I am decidedly of opinion that the decrees of Providence are at all times wisest and best.'

THE RACE WAS OVER! The cannon were fired once again. England sighed with relief that after all she would not be ruled by a series of geriatric monarchs. The Crown of England would not adorn the bald or wigged heads of George III's twelve children. Instead now it would zigzag: first go horizontally from the

Regent to the Duke of York, to the Duke of Clarence, to the
Duke of Kent and then descend down to the next generation, to
the newest Royal baby (soon to be christened and known as
Victoria), and if she died it would revert to the Duke of Cumberland; failing him having any sons it would go sideways again to
the Duke of Cambridge and his son.

The Duke wrote: '. . . my little girl is I am delighted to say
strong and healthy; too healthy, I fear, in the opinion of some
members of my family, by whom she is regarded as an intruder.'

So precious was this child that the Duchess of Kent breast-fed
her, or as the Duke said 'gave her maternal nutriment', instead of
recruiting a wet nurse as was then usual.

★   ★   ★

A few weeks later Dr Siebold went by coach back to Germany
for the confinement of the Duchess of Kent's brother's second
child. The baby, Prince Albert of Saxe-Coburg, was born on 26
August. Twenty-two years later he was to be yet another passen-
ger on the Royal yacht to the Royal altar. The Coburgs were to
take over from the House of Hanover after all.

★   ★   ★

Prince Leopold, when King of the Belgians, often assured his
niece, Queen Victoria, that 'Uncle King', when Regent, had done
all he could to prevent her being born in England. 'Arrived in
London, we were very unkindly treated by George IV whose
great wish was to get you and your mama out of the country,' he
told her. And he wrote: 'I know not what would have become
of you and your mama if I then had existed no longer. George IV
hated your father . . . He did all to prevent you being born in
England.'

★   ★   ★

George IV hated christenings and funerals – reminders that
soon someone else would be sitting in *his* throne. He also hated
the Coburg family, dubbing Prince Leopold 'the Marquis peu à
peu' and his sister, Kent's wife, 'the Swiss governess'.

[154]

It was the latter hatred overcoming the former that dragged him along to the Cupola Room in Kensington Palace where, a month after her birth, the latest Coburg child was to be christened. He had after all been appointed her godfather, together with the Tsar of Russia for whom Princess Lieven was present as proxy.

A letter had already been sent to the Regent submitting names for his approval – GEORGINA CHARLOTTE AUGUSTA ALEXANDRINA VICTORIA. But it was not until the eve of the actual christening that the Regent sent a message to the Kents 'that the name of Georgina could not be used – as He did not chuse to place His name before the Emperor of Russia's – and He could not allow it to follow'. The new self-importance of the Kents, as parents and guardians of the heir to the throne, was deflated – the Regent thought that they were too impatient to wait their turn. But they cannot have been surprised, as Lord Melbourne was later to tell Queen Victoria that she had been named after the Tsar specially to annoy the Regent, who 'HATED him; God damn him!'

Surrounded by all this hate and envy, the baby Princess lay in the lawn-sleeved arms of the Archbishop of Canterbury who stood beside the golden font waiting for the Prince Regent to give a name. The Regent remained silent for a long time.

'Alexandrina,' he finally and gruffly muttered.

The Duke suggested another name might be added. 'Charlotte?' The Regent shook his head at the mention of his dead daughter.

'Augusta?' suggested Kent, a little angrily.

Again the Regent shook his head; he did not care for its innuendoes of grandeur. He did not care for present company either. Perhaps he sensed that these Coburgs would someday take over from the House of Hanover.

'Elizabeth?' suggested the exasperated Kent.

Again the Regent did not approve. The Duchess was now beginning to cry. The Archbishop was looking from Prince to Prince and wondering if he would ever put down his burden.

There was another long silence only broken by the Duchess's sobbing.

'Well, what's her mother's name?' thundered the Regent at

last. 'Let her be called after her mother. But Alexandrina must come first.'

So, to Kent's fury, his child was christened Alexandrina Victoria. For the first nine years of her life she was known as Drina. The Duke of Clarence later suggested that the sailors would think she was named after Nelson's flagship, *The Victory*.

*   *   *

The Princess prospered. Eight months after her birth the Duke of Kent died. He had gone for a walk and when he returned 'his boots soaked through with the wet'. He did not change his damp socks and caught a fatal chill.

The Duke would have been proud of his daughter, the Great White Queen, and he would have been so pleased to see her bathroom at Osborne, on the Isle of Wight, where a framed notice quoted Wesley: 'Cleanliness is Next to Godliness'. The Duke of Kent so very much wanted everything and everyone to be tidy – and clean.

*   *   *

Shortly after Victoria's birth, the Duchess of Cumberland was delivered a fine baby boy. There were now three heirs for the three kingdoms. Princess Victoria of Kent was first, Prince George of Cumberland was second and Prince George of Cambridge was third. Victoria was, of course, to come to the throne of England nineteen years later, where she would remain for sixty-four years. But in the long run the youngest and best of the sons of George III could claim his victory too. Those nice Cambridges shared the throne with those nasty Kents when their grand-daughter, Princess Mary of Teck, married George V. Their grand-daughter is the present Queen. ('For many that are first are last and last first.')

Princess Elizabeth and the Prince of Hesse-Homburg had no offspring of their own but Elizabeth gave all children a gift: she founded a model works' kindergarten. Her creche in Hanover founded for the small children of 'those who go out to work for the day' have multiplied.

[156]

*   *   *

The Prince Regent who became King George IV in January 1820 on the death of his mad father did not have to worry about the 'vilest wretch on earth' becoming Queen. He locked her out of Westminster Abbey during his Coronation so she could not be crowned Queen of England. Five days later she died of constipation in Hammersmith. It was announced that she had 'an obstruction of the bowels, attended with inflammation'. Doctors prescribed bleeding, opium, calomel and so much castor oil that Lord Brougham said it 'would have turned the stomach of a horse'. She died.

At last the Regent was free to marry. Instead he fell in love with Lady Conyngham – a fat jolly old thing of fifty-two. She was nicknamed the 'Vice-Queen'.

*   *   *

And so the Coburgs came to the throne and they have all lived happily ever after.

George III's determination succeeded. His aim for his Teutonic family to be Royally the most pure and most glorious on earth succeeded, in a way; six marriage-manacled generations and two centuries later, the Queen of England, Elizabeth II, heads a family which almost fulfils his prayer. Since 1772 the blood royal of the sovereign has been tainted only once with that of a subject: the Queen's mother, Lady Elizabeth Bowes-Lyon. She is the only British Queen to share a throne since Henry VIII's last wife, Katharine Parr, 1547 – 1553, who had no children. Although James II's wife, Ann Hyde, was mother of Mary II and Queen Anne, she died before her husband came to the throne.

Whether the Royal Marriages Act was right may be disputed, but the Queen shows its beneficial effect on monarch-breeding. George III's attempt to impose what scientists would now call a system of eugenics on the family has had good results. No family has had such an elevated position or been the target of such world-wide adulation. George III laid the foundation stone for the most resilient dynasty in history – the House of Coburg. It is still the House of Coburg, but by a different appellation. Because of anti-German feeling during the First World War, the name was changed from Coburg to that of the family's medieval castle, Windsor. George V also abandoned all his German honours and insisted that all his relatives living in England took British titles. The throne has emerged triumphant; England may not be so great any longer but the monarch is.

And George III's descendants still dominate the caste of royalty. His descendants have occupied the Imperial thrones of Germany and Russia, ruled over Greece, Yugoslavia and Roumania and still reign in Norway, Sweden, Denmark and Spain as well as in Britain.

George III is still winning.

*   *   *

Appendix
The Houses

Winner or loser, good or evil, the participants of the Royal race all had the same fate: death. Some of the English houses, though, have had a more durable fate than the people they sheltered.

CLAREMONT, where Princess Charlotte died in 1817, is now a boarding school for the daughters of Christian Scientists. It is open to the public the first weekend or first Sunday in every month from February through to November.

Admission: 25p adults, 10p children. Trains to Claygate Station (on Waterloo-Guildford, via Cobham line) thence taxi or 206 bus to Claremont Gates. The room in which Charlotte gave birth to her dead Prince is now the study of the headmistress.

CARLTON HOUSE was demolished in 1826. Carlton House Terrace was built on the site – a row of aristocratic mansions divided by the sweeping Duke of York's steps which are surmounted by a memorial to the Duke. This column was paid for by retaining one day's pay from every soldier between the ranks of drummer boy and major-general. The columns from the entrance of Carlton House were reused in the portico at the National Gallery.

BUCKINGHAM HOUSE became Buckingham Palace after Queen Charlotte's death in 1819, and extensive additions were carried out by the architect, John Nash. It was one of the first houses in the world to use steel construction. Although it is not open to the public anyone who tells a policeman at the gate that they want to sign Her Majesty's Visitors' Book will be able to walk across the courtyard and be ushered into a small room inside the palace where a footman will watch as the book is signed. Free.

The chapel was rebuilt as an art gallery after it was bombed in the last war and here a rotation of works from the fabulous Royal art collection is shown to the public.

On Wednesday and Thursday afternoons the Royal Mews at the south-west corner are open to the public where the old coaches as well as the new horses can be seen.

ROYAL SOVEREIGN A few decorative remains of the yacht which

APPENDIX

took the brides across the Channel are in the Naval museum at Portsmouth.

KENSINGTON PALACE where George II died and where Queen Victoria was born is still used as apartments for the sovereign's relatives: Princess Margaret, the Duke of Kent, and Princess Alice. The State Apartments and suite occupied by Princess Victoria are open.

ST JAMES'S PALACE Members of the Royal Family and high-ranking members of the Royal household have apartments now in this Tudor palace. The splendid Chapel Royal may only be seen during Matins on winter Sundays – like the rest of the palace, it was designed by Holbein. The choristers still wear Tudor uniforms of scarlet and gold.

KEW Still only a penny entrance fee to the 300 acres of gardens which are open every day except Christmas Day. Queen Charlotte's cottage, where the guests had tea after the Kent/Clarence wedding, will be open to the public again after Easter 1978. The Dutch House, where the Dukes of Kent and Clarence were married, is open to the public from Easter Monday every year to mid-September and costs 25p entrance fee for adults. Cambridge Cottage is now the Wood and Tree Museum. King's Cottage is now the over-plushed home of the managing director of an advertising agency.

BUSHEY, near Hampton Court Palace. The much-loved home of the Duke of Clarence and his ten bastard children became the headquarters of the National Standards Laboratory in 1901 and is now known as the National Physical Laboratory. The park, but not the house, is open to the public.

BRIGHTON PAVILION now continues its role as a pleasure palace and is open all the year round to tourists. It has been carefully kept as the Regent devised it except that his huge bath with taps which gushed forth heated sea water has been concreted over to make way for the busy kiosk and souvenir shop.

STEINE HOUSE, Brighton Mrs Fitzherbert's mansion is now a hostel of the Y.M.C.A.

WINDSOR CASTLE still dominates the castles of England and is still used as a home by the Royal Family. Tickets are available for the state apartments. Old Master drawings and Queen Mary's dolls' house. In St George's Chapel there is a statue of Prince Leopold and an ornate memorial to poor Princess Charlotte showing her rising with her dead baby to heaven.

[160]